Cesar Chavez

Cesar Chavez

LABOR LEADER

DAVID SEIDMAN

FRANKLIN WATTS
A Division of Scholastic Inc.
New York Toronto London Auckland Sydney
Mexico City New Delhi Hong Kong
Danbury, Connecticut

To Allison Littleton, who's fought her own workplace battles.

ACKNOWLEDGMENTS

Many thanks to Wendy Mead, the editor who hired me for this project, and Paul Levine, my lawyer, who looked out for me in negotiating the contract.

Photographs © 2004: AP/Wide World Photos: 113 (Damian Dovarganes), 62; TM/© the Cesar E. Chavez Foundation, www.chavezfoundation.org: 10, 14, 21, 22, 44; Corbis Images: 33, 70, 77, 92, 106 (Bettmann), 102 (Jeff Franko/Bettmann), 18 (Dorothea Lange), 65 (Ted Streshinsky), 38, 59 (UPI), 96 (Ron Watts); Stockphoto.com/Victor Aleman: cover background, back cover; Take Stock: 56, 57 (George Ballis), 90 (Bob Fitch); Time Life Pictures/Getty Images: 84 (Bill Eppridge), cover foreground, 2 (Arthur Schatz), 73; Walter P. Reuther Library, Wayne State University: 60 (Harvey Richards), 36, 42, 45, 50, 74, 80, 81, 88, 89, 91, 98.

Library of Congress Cataloging-in-Publication Data

Seidman, David.
  Cesar Chavez : labor leader / by David Seidman.
    p. cm. — (Great life stories)

Summary: Discusses the life and work of Cesar Chavez, an American labor leader who organized the farm worker's union, United Farm Workers.

Includes bibliographical references and index.

ISBN 0-531-12319-7

1. Chavez, Cesar, 1927—Juvenile literature. 2. United Farm Workers—History—Juvenile literature. 3. Migrant agricultural laborers—Labor unions—United States—Officials and employees—Biography—Juvenile literature. 4. Labor leaders—United States—Biography—Juvenile literature. [1. Chavez, Cesar, 1927- 2. Labor leaders. 3. Mexican Americans—Biography. 4. Migrant labor. 5. United Farm Workers.] I. Title. II. Series.

  HD6509.C48S45 2003
  331.88'13'092—dc22

2003013345

Contents

Planting the Seeds

Cesar Chavez was nobody. Small, shy, poorly educated, and very poor, he was a farmworker like thousands of others, trudging from field to field when he could get work and nearly starving when he couldn't. At twenty-five years old, he had three children and a pregnant wife, and little chance of giving them anything better than the poverty and aching overwork that he himself had endured since age eleven. He and other farmworkers had no power to get better wages, safe and healthy working conditions, or anything else from their employers.

Nevertheless, Chavez turned himself into a world-famous leader, a friend of presidential candidates, and a hero to Latinos, liberals, and laborers. He built the first successful, long-lasting union of farmworkers and broke the will of powerful corporations. He even fought his own supporters and starved himself almost to death in order to hold their loyalty. Long after his death, his work has remained an example of what one determined man can do, even if the man seems like a nobody.

INTO THE NIGHT

Chavez's story starts before he was born with a man fleeing into darkness. In 1880, Cesario Chavez, nicknamed Papa Chayo, was a *peón* (from the Spanish word for pawn)—a Mexican farmworker living nearly as a slave under plantation owners who held enormous power over the government. In the state of Chihuahua, where Cesario lived, the power belonged to the Terrazas family. According to Chavez family legend, Cesario was furious with a grower's son about an injustice (no one remembers what it was). To get rid of the troublemaker, the Terrazas family wanted to draft Cesario into the army.

No one wants to be drafted. If Cesario had wanted to join the army, he could have enlisted, but draftees joined only because the government ordered them to. Even worse, Cesario had a good chance of being killed in the army. In October 1880, for instance, Apache Indians fought the army near the area where Cesario lived, and possibly in his town.

Fortunately for Cesario, he heard about the plan to draft him, and he escaped into the night and out of the country. He settled among southern Arizona's deserts and mountains. He worked as a freight hauler, driving mules that carried ores from the area's mines. He had escaped so fast that he'd left his wife Dorotea (nicknamed Mama Tella) and children behind. Within a few years, he brought them to Arizona, where his son Librado joined him on the mule train. By the start of the twentieth century, though, Cesario had bigger plans.

HOMESTEAD

"It was all tumbleweed and mesquite and ugliness," *Washington Post* journalist Paul Hendrickson wrote more than a century later in describing the North Gila River Valley. The valley lies in Arizona's southwest corner, near California and northeast of the city of Yuma. Cesario irrigated the parched soil and turned it into a 160-acre (65-hectare) vegetable farm.

Papa Chayo and Mama Tella's children eventually started their own families and left the farm—all but the quiet, devoted Librado. In 1924, when he was thirty-eight years old and still living in his father's house, he married "a very tiny woman, little more than five feet tall, with a slender waist and delicate features framed by long black hair."

That was the grown-up Cesar Chavez's description of Juana Estrada. Her family had moved from Mexico to the United States in 1892, when she was about six months old. Said Cesar, "She talked a lot, her tongue skipping as fast as her mind from one thing to another."

Their daughter Rita was born in 1925. To support the growing family, Librado bought a small complex of nearby buildings that housed a grocery store, a garage, and a pool hall. With more than a dozen brothers and sisters producing plenty of children, he had a lot of steady customers.

Librado and Juana kept a home inside the store. There, on March 31, 1927, they had the second of their five children: Cesario Estrada Chavez.

In October of 1929, before little Cesario turned three years old, the economy of the United States collapsed, and the Great Depression began. Within two months, the number of people in the country without jobs rose from 700,000 to more than 3,000,000. By the end of 1933, the number of jobless grew to more than eight million.

Librado had been letting his customers buy goods on credit and pay for them later. When they lost their jobs, they stopped paying. In 1932, Librado had to sell his businesses and move his family onto Papa Chayo's farm—or, rather, the farm that used to be Papa Chayo's. The old man was now dead, and Librado moved his brood into the farmhouse's north wing, a storeroom that Papa Chayo had used for storing corn, pumpkins, and other crops.

THE BEST YEARS

The room was small, but the farm was large. Cesario climbed its trees with his younger brother Richard (born in 1929) and his cousin Manuel, played in the pasture, and imagined that the cracks in their room's walls and ceiling formed the outlines of animals and people. The house had no electricity or running water, but because of the farm, the family had plenty of

This photograph shows a young Cesario with a friend. The Great Depression would dramatically affect his childhood.

food. Cesario loved living there and remembered it warmly for the rest of his life. "We had been poor," he told interviewer Studs Terkel decades later, "but we knew every night that there was a bed there [for us]."

By 1935, there were five Chavez children: Cesario, his sister Rita, his younger brother Richard, his sister Vicky (born in 1933), and the last and youngest, Lenny (born in 1934). Their parents worked hard to raise them properly.

Juana was full of *dichos* (sayings and mottos). About violence, for instance, she told Cesario, "It's best to turn the other cheek [rather than fight]. God gave you senses like eyes and mind and tongue, and you can get out of anything." It was an unusual stance to take in a culture in which a man who didn't fight was considered weak.

Librado spoke more with his actions than with words. "Unlike most Mexicans [in those days]," said journalist Peter Matthiessen, "Mr. Chavez never considered it unmanly to bathe his children or take them to the toilet or do small menial jobs around the house."

Mama Tella contributed too. Though she was more than ninety years old and could barely see, Cesario's grandmother instructed the children in the Catholic faith and prayed much of the day. Her training had power: Chavez was a firm Catholic all his life.

For his nonreligious education, Cesario went to school. He hated it. He was a Mexican American, also known as a Chicano, and white students called Chicanos "dirty Mexicans." When Cesario or other Chicano students spoke Spanish, teachers scolded them and sometimes whacked their knuckles with a ruler.

It was one of those teachers who first called the little boy by the slightly Americanized name "Cesar" rather than the more traditionally

Down on the Farm

By the time Librado Chavez came to California, the state had become an agricultural powerhouse—and a source of abuse for farmworkers and Latinos.

California had been part of Mexico until the United States fought the Mexican-American War of 1846–1848. In defeating Mexico, the United States won a huge swath of territory that included California. Shortly after the war ended, a northern California construction foreman named James Marshall discovered gold in the region. Over the next several months, thousands of people flocked to California.

A group of men who owned vast tracts of California land recognized that the new settlers would need to buy food and that people living elsewhere would buy it too. The landowners established large farms primarily growing fruit and wheat. They needed farmhands and got them from the vast agricultural regions of Asia—first from China, then from Japan. They paid the immigrants low wages and worked them hard and long. Things got so bad that, during 1884, Chinese pickers of hop (a plant used to make beer) in southern California's Kern County staged a walkout against their employers. Unfortunately for the pickers, the walkout didn't force the growers into making many changes.

When the unhappy Asians left the West Coast for other parts of the country, native-born Americans resented having to compete with them for work. As a result, Congress passed the Chinese Exclusion Act of 1882 to keep additional Chinese people out of the country. In the early 1900s, an agreement between the United States and Japan limited Japanese immigration as well.

As Asian workers aged or died, immigrants from Mexico replaced them. The growers treated the Mexicans no better than they had treated the Asians. During 1903, hundreds of Japanese and Mexican farmworkers toiling in the beet fields south of Kern County formed a union to demand higher wages. The growers refused, and the union collapsed.

Hispanic "Cesario," according to Rita. The teacher also wanted him to sit with children his own age, but Cesar insisted on sitting with his older sister. He simply refused to move, and eventually the teacher let him stay. A few days later, he decided to join his peers, but he had found a successful tactic to help him get his way that would make him famous: a nonviolent but stubborn refusal to obey authority.

DRY TIMES

In 1933, a drought hit southwestern Arizona. The Chavez farm's crops shriveled and died, and the ground was too dry to plant new ones. Librado couldn't pay his debts, which amounted to $4,080. He applied for a loan from Archibald Griffin, a banker who was also his neighbor.

Griffin turned him down. On August 29, 1937, the state government took over the farm. The loss would have been hard to take at any time, but it hit when the family was already suffering. Only a few weeks earlier, Mama Tella had died.

At age ten, Cesar Chavez saw the happiest period of his life end. The state let the Chavez family live on the farm for another year but wouldn't let them use it to earn a living. Librado left his family and went on the road, hoping to make enough money to buy the farm back.

After months of struggle, he found work threshing (separating seeds from pods) in bean fields near the southern California town of Oxnard, more than 300 miles (about 500 kilometers) northwest of the Chavez farm. He invited Juana and the children to join him. In the late summer of 1938, they did.

"[Our life] all of a sudden changed," Chavez told Studs Terkel thirty years later. "When you're small, you can't figure these things out. You know something's not right, and you don't like it, but you don't question it, and you don't let [it] get you down."

ONE BAD *BARRIO*

The Chavez family moved into La Colonia (Spanish for "The Colony"), a violent *barrio* (Hispanic neighborhood) on Oxnard's eastern edge. The place was densely crowded and filthy. The homes had outhouses instead of indoor bathrooms, and no sewers to carry waste away. It was one of the toughest, most dangerous neighborhoods in town and was especially unsafe at night, because it had no streetlights.

The Chavez family lived in an old wooden shed with dirt floors. On Cesar's first night in Oxnard, he left his toys outside, as he always had in Arizona. Overnight, someone stole them, leaving Cesar shocked and confused.

After losing the farm, the Chavez family left their hometown and went to work in the fields.

The Chavezes were so poor that the children had to walk to school barefoot. After school, Cesar and his siblings helped their parents harvest walnuts. Cesar hated the job. "The workers would shake the nuts loose from the trees with long, rough poles with metal hooks," writes Consuelo Rodriguez in her book *Cesar Chavez*. "It was a backbreaking job, but the harder part, for some, was picking the nuts off the ground, one by one, bent over at the waist for hour after hour."

After a few months, Oxnard's harvest ended. The Chavez family roamed from field to field, looking for work. When they found it, they stayed in labor camps. The camps were fields where farmers dumped their workers to spend the night. Some of them provided housing— rough plaster shacks without light, heat, or running water—but nearly all the camps were filthy, uncomfortable, and overcrowded.

Fortunately, the Chavezes had one last chance to repair their lives. On February 6, 1939, the state of Arizona auctioned off their farm. If they could raise enough money, they could buy it back.

They couldn't raise the money. The buyer—who paid the bargain price of $1,750—was Archibald Griffin. It seemed that he had been eyeing the farm for himself all along. Eleven-year-old Cesar watched Griffin's tractor rip up the farm's trees. Helpless and frustrated, Cesar felt that like the trees, he and his family were being uprooted.

MIGRANT LIFE

Cesar's father had heard that farmers needed helpers to pick peas near Atascadero, a town in central California. Off they went to look for work, competing with hundreds of thousands of others.

The Chavezes arrived in Atascadero in mid-June of 1939, but the harvest had already ended. Following another rumor, they traveled about 100 miles (160 km) north to the wine-making town Gonzales. The growers there didn't need them, either; Gonzales appeared overstocked with workers. A farm-labor recruiter told the Chavezes to show up for pea-picking in Half Moon Bay, another 100 miles (about 160 km) up the coast.

There was indeed work in Half Moon Bay, but also some nasty details that the recruiter had failed to mention. Harvest workers did "piecework"—they were paid for the number of peas that they picked. Half Moon Bay paid about half the rate that the recruiter had promised, and the bosses counted only the best peas for payment and threw away the rest. For their first day's work, the entire Chavez family earned 20 cents.

The Chavezes heard that fields about 50 miles (80 km) east of Half Moon Bay, near the city of San Jose, needed cherry pickers. After finding a place to live in the crowded, brutal San Jose barrio Sal Si Puedes ("Get Out If You Can") they found that the cherry orchards did need pickers. The need lasted only two weeks, but once it ended, other orchards nearby were hiring.

Over the next few years, the family traveled the state in search of work. By late May, the family would be working in Oxnard's sweltering bean fields or in the high-altitude southern California towns of Hemet picking cherries and Beaumont picking apricots. Early summer brought more apricots, in Moorpark (about 20 miles [30 km] northeast of Oxnard) or San Jose. Midsummer meant looking for work picking chili peppers, corn, and lima beans. In late summer and early fall, the family sought jobs picking cucumbers, grapes, plums, and tomatoes in the heat of central California's San Joaquin Valley.

The coming of cold weather meant moving a few hundred miles south to Brawley and other small farm towns in the Imperial Valley, near Mexico. There the Chavez family picked carrots, peas, and mustard.

Unions for All . . . Almost

For years, U.S. workers had been treated unfairly and saw no way to improve the situation. Employers could cut their wages at any time, force them to work in unsafe conditions, or make them labor without a break for hours on end. When workers banded together into unions to negotiate for better working conditions, employers often ignored them and even fired them. If the workers went on strike, the employers could call the police to beat and arrest them. In some areas, the local government declared it illegal for workers to organize themselves.

On July 5, 1935, though, President Franklin D. Roosevelt signed the National Labor Relations Act. The new law allowed workers to form unions and hold strikes. In the words of the act, "It shall be an unfair labor practice for an employer . . . to dominate or interfere with the formation or administration of any labor organization . . . to encourage or discourage membership in any labor organization . . . [and] to refuse to bargain collectively with the representatives of his employees."

But for farmworkers, there was a catch. "[In this law,] the term 'employee'. . . shall not include any individual employed as an agricultural laborer." In other words, farmworkers had no right to form unions. For years afterwards, Cesar Chavez and many other farm labor leaders would fight to get the same rights as other workers.

From October to Christmas, there was cotton picking. It was painfully difficult work, but little else grew at that cold time of year. December through March could mean harvesting broccoli, a job that sometimes required Cesar to wade in freezing mud and water.

January might bring work picking cabbage and lettuce. The first three months of a year might also offer work picking cauliflower, mustard greens, or onions, while spring brought melon harvests. There were other crops, too, such as figs—"the milk of the fig eats through your skin like acid," Chavez said in his memoirs—and beets. "That was work for an animal, not a man. . . . Stooping and digging all day, and the beets are heavy—oh, that's brutal work."

UNIONS AND POLITICS

The late 1930s showed Cesar Chavez a glimpse of his future. In 1937, the Congress of Industrial Organizations, a giant family of unions, had formed UCAPAWA—the United Cannery, Agricultural, Packing and

Harvesting crops is backbreaking work. Here a Mexican woman works in an onion field.

Allied Workers of America. Librado quickly joined, as did his brother and fellow farmworker Valeriano. "Sometimes the men would meet at our house, and I remember seeing their picket signs and hearing them talk," the grown-up Cesar Chavez told historian Eugene Nelson. "They had a strike, and my father and uncle picketed."

Unfortunately, Chavez said, "They lost the strike, and that was the end of the union." Nevertheless, the family didn't quit. "We were probably one of the strikingest families in California," Chavez said in a 1991 speech. His father eagerly joined union after union, but none of them improved workers' lives much—a fact that young Cesar never forgot.

Cesar's mother, meanwhile, was almost dangerously generous. "On the road, no matter how badly off we were, she would never let us pass a guy or family in trouble," Cesar told the Associated Press news service in 1991. Juana Chavez gave people whatever she had. "That's why we suffered so much. But my mother would tell us, 'You always have to help the needy, and God will help you.'"

The family constantly faced racism. The storefronts of restaurants and other public places carried signs reading "No Dogs or Mexicans Allowed." In Brawley, the police wouldn't let Mexican Americans set foot in the whites' part of town.

Because his family was migrating from town to town, Cesar Chavez attended as many as thirty different schools. He was disappointed that his education was so spotty, and as an adult encouraged his children and followers to get good schooling and college degrees. Not only was his education haphazard, but some of the schools he attended were segregated, putting Chicano students in separate and inferior classrooms.

No Mexicans Wanted

Throughout the Southwest, businesses and other organizations owned by whites kept Chicanos and other Latinos out. They refused to give jobs to Latinos or rent homes to them. The problem was especially obvious in schools. Because many Latino children spoke Spanish before they learned English, white school administrators said that they had a "language handicap" and placed them in separate rooms or even separate buildings. The white students got better teachers, classrooms, and other educational resources. While schools for white students taught math and literature, schools for Latinos taught cooking, cleaning, and other skills for servants.

Not every town was so harsh. Lemon Grove, a small California farm town south of Hemet and west of Brawley, allowed Chicano students to attend the mostly white Lemon Grove Grammar School. Eventually, though, the school board grew uncomfortable with the Chicanos and told Principal Jerome Green to get rid of them. On Monday, January 5, 1931, the school's seventy-five Chicano students returned to school after a New Year's break to find Green standing in the school's doorway, blocking them from entering. He told them that the school board had given them a new school, but in the words of one student, "It wasn't a school. It was an old building. Everyone called it La Caballeriza (the barnyard)."

The next month, the children's parents sued. In the name of twelve-year-old student Roberto Alvarez, they filed *Roberto Alvarez* v. *The Board of Trustees of the Lemon Grove School District*.

On March 30, the parents won. Superior Court Judge Claude Chambers declared, "To separate all the Mexicans in one group can only be done by infringing [breaking] the laws." The school board returned the Chicano students to Lemon Grove Grammar School. It was the first time that a U.S. court had ruled that school segregation was illegal.

Teachers and students made fun of Cesar for his poor command of English. At one school, a teacher hung a sign around his neck that read "I am a clown, I speak Spanish." Cesar struck back by ridiculing the whites' speech, calling English a "dog language." The nonviolent ways of his parents may have been the only thing that kept him from lashing out physically.

Cesar did have other outlets for his energy. He was a mischievous kid. In Oxnard, he persuaded Richard to stick his finger in a light socket, giving the boy a shock that sent him yelling. In Summerland, a beach town about 40 miles (64 km) up the coast from Oxnard, an uncle took away some beer that Cesar and his cousin Manuel wanted to drink. They got even by putting laxative in the uncle's food. Cesar's prankishness wouldn't last, though. By the 1940s, he was becoming a man.

Cesar, shown here in a school photo, was picked on in class by teachers and students alike.

This is Chavez's eighth grade graduation photograph. While he looks calm and quiet here, he was a rebellious teenager.

The Wanderer

As Chavez became a teenager, his urge to misbehave and his childhood stubbornness transformed into a strong will that bordered on defiance. He wasn't rude or impudent, but he quietly developed his own convictions. His mother used herbs and folk remedies to treat illnesses; Cesar preferred doctors. He rejected the old-fashioned mariachi music that his parents liked and listened to bandleaders such as Duke Ellington and Benny Goodman, who played fast dance music that teenagers loved.

Chavez asserted himself further by becoming a *pachuco*, part of a group of slick-dressing young Latino men. *Pachucos* wore zoot suits, as did young African Americans, Filipinos, and others. A favorite outfit of the hippest musicians, the zoot suit was a getup with baggy pants that got tight at the ankles, thick-soled shoes, and extra-long jackets.

Many people didn't trust *pachucos*. "Some authority figures had condemned zoot suits as the garb of gangsters and hoodlums," according to the *Los Angeles Times's* Mary Rourke. In farm communities, police officers harassed Chavez and his friends. In the wine-country town of Merced, for instance, officers forced them to take off their fancy shoes and gave them ten minutes to get out of town.

During 1942, fifteen-year-old Cesar Chavez performed his greatest act of defiance to date. He quit school. Earlier that year, Librado was injured in a car accident and could not work. To support the family,

The Zoot Suit Riots

During 1943, *pachucos* like Chavez became a nationally famous symbol and target of bigotry. In early June, a gang of Los Angeles *pachucos* beat up a group of eleven white U.S. Navy sailors who were on leave. The incident infuriated white citizens and led to anti-*pachuco* riots. California historian Carey McWilliams wrote that on June 7, "Marching through the streets of downtown Los Angeles, a mob of several thousand soldiers, sailors, and civilians proceeded to beat up every zoot suiter they could find." Even the police joined in. They publicly stripped the clothes off of anyone wearing a zoot suit, pounded them bloody with their nightsticks, and jailed them.

The rioting continued for days and ended only after the navy declared downtown Los Angeles off limits to sailors. The only people arrested for the rampage were some of its *pachuco* victims. The incident shocked the country, although many white Californians felt the *pachucos* were to blame.

Chavez worked full-time in the fields. His mother didn't like it, but the young man held firm.

MEETING HELEN

In early 1943, the Chavez family was heading south through central California. After the family members made camp in a tent city, fifteen-year-old Chavez left to look around Delano, a nearby grape-growing hamlet of about six thousand people. He quickly found a malt shop, La Baratita ("the little cheap one"), filled with teenagers. One was a small girl with flowers in her hair. Her name was Helen Fabela.

Helen, a few months younger than Chavez, had been born in Brawley to farmworker parents. Like Chavez, she'd traveled up and down California picking produce. By 1943, though, her family had stopped migrating and settled in Delano. She was better educated than Chavez because she attended the local high school. Helen also had more money than he did because she worked after school at the People's Market grocery store, down the street from La Baratita.

Chavez was too shy to ask Helen out on a date. Instead, he became a steady customer at People's. For their first date, "she asked me to a show," he told his children. Because Chavez had no spare cash, Helen paid for the evening. From then on, they dated whenever he was in Delano.

GETTING SHIPSHAPE

In 1944, at age seventeen, Cesar Chavez performed another act of independence. Against his parents' wishes, he enlisted in the navy. He actually didn't want to enlist, but he knew that like other young men, he'd soon be drafted into the army. He didn't want to join the army, though he never publicly explained why. In any event, he felt that the safest way to avoid being drafted into the army was to join the navy, like his cousin Manuel, who had enlisted months earlier. Mainly, though, he enlisted to escape the endless, sweaty, boring farmwork.

In his memoirs, Cesar called his time in the navy the worst two years of his life. In his opinion, the navy treated its sailors as mindless pieces of equipment, ordering them from place to place, rigidly regimenting their actions, and creating a life that seemed worse than a prison sentence.

He nearly learned about prison firsthand in 1944. While in Delano on leave from the navy, he went to a movie. The theater restricted Latinos to the right side of the auditorium. Before enlisting in the navy, he would have sat where he was told. Something inside him had changed, though. It may have been that in the navy, he'd seen people stand up to discrimination. "I saw this white kid fighting because someone had called him a polack, and I found out he was Polish and hated that word," he later remembered.

In any event, "the devil must have got in me," Chavez told the *Washington Post*'s Paul Hendrickson twenty-five years later. Although he was scared, "I just got up and went over to the left side."

The theater's manager called the police, who held Chavez but didn't arrest him, apparently because he hadn't broken any laws. After about an hour, the officer in charge lectured Chavez in an attempt to scare him into obedience and then let him go. The incident showed Chavez the power of nonviolent action.

JOB TO JOB TO JOB

World War II ended in 1945. In 1946, the navy discharged Chavez. He went back to the farmwork that he had joined the navy to escape.

Conditions for farmworkers were as bad as ever, partly because local governments sided with growers. In 1945, the federal Department of Labor issued Bureau of Labor Statistics Bulletin 836, which was a report on farmworkers. It quoted a deputy sheriff from the region that included Delano as saying, "We protect our farmers here in Kern County. . . . They put us in here and they can put us out again, so we serve them. But the Mexicans are trash. They have no standard of living. We herd them like pigs."

The growers made sure that the Mexican farmworkers lived like pigs too. "If we were thirsty, we brought our own water because water was seldom provided," said Marcus Lopez, a farmworker in the 1940s who became a college professor. "When we needed the use of a toilet, we had to squat discreetly to relieve ourselves, behind some bush or tree or a nearby field, while our co-workers, men and women, politely looked away."

Though growers skimped on anything that would help their workers, they didn't mind spending money on other items. The late 1940s saw the development of new and very deadly poisons that the growers sprayed on their crops to kill insects. DDT (short for dichlorodiphenyltrichloroethane) not only killed bugs but also may cause cancer in humans. Methyl bromide poisoned farmworkers by making their bodies' chemical reactions go haywire, producing too much of some fluids and not enough of others. Parathion could weaken lungs and other body parts until it caused death. Even when they didn't kill, these pesticides

Workers and Unions

The late 1940s were a tough time for organized labor. In 1947, Congress passed the Taft-Hartley Act, which limited the power of labor unions to sign up all the workers in a company, and forced unions to give employers sixty days' notice before launching a strike.

Farmworkers in the southwestern states had an additional problem. After the United States entered World War II, plenty of farmworkers, such as Chavez, left the fields for military service or factory jobs making military supplies, which paid better than farmwork. Farmers complained that they didn't have enough hands to raise and harvest crops. Meanwhile, Mexico had too many unemployed workers.

The solution was to bring in *braceros*, from the Spanish word *brazo*, which means "arm." *Braceros* were Mexican farmworkers that the U.S. government delivered to American growers. The *braceros* came by the thousands and worked for less money than native farmworkers. Growers liked the system so much that the government renewed it even after farmworkers such as Chavez came back from the war. In 1949 alone, more than 100,000 *braceros* were working U.S. fields.

For a union to work well, it has to sign up most or all of the workforce. The *bracero* system added so many people to the fields that signing up most of the workforce was nearly impossible. To have any strength, a union has to keep its members ready to stand up against employers. The *braceros* were so desperate for work that many of them weren't ready to fight the employers.

It seemed as though farmworkers like Chavez could never improve their living situations.

and others caused vomiting, stomach cramps, diarrhea, headaches, convulsions, birth defects, and other problems.

Chavez wanted to change the situation. He joined a union, sometimes called the National Agricultural Workers Union and sometimes the National Farm Labor Union. When the union called for a walkout to protest working conditions, he joined it. "A union leader got up and started talking to all the workers about 'the cause.' I would have died right then if someone had told me how and why to die for our cause. But no one did. There was a crisis and a mob, but there was no organization, and nothing came of it all."

Chavez had something other than labor activism on his mind. Since he had gotten out of the navy, he and Helen had been dating seriously. On October 22, 1948, the twenty-one-year-old Chavez and Helen got married.

The groom spent the next few years drifting from job to job. At first, the newlyweds lived in Delano, where Chavez picked grapes and cotton. The couple moved to San Jose, where Chavez's parents and his brother Richard were working in strawberry and apricot fields, and settled in Sal Si Puedes.

They also began to have children. Their first, Fernando, was born in 1949. Their daughter Sylvia was born in the early months of the following year, and their second daughter, Linda, was born in January of 1951.

By that time, Chavez had left San Jose and moved the family to the forest town of Crescent City, more than 400 miles (about 650 km) to the north. Along with Richard and their cousin Manuel, Chavez had found work in nearby lumberyards.

Although Chavez found the woods restful, Crescent City received nearly five times the rainfall of San Jose. It was too much for Chavez and his family. In 1952, they returned to Sal Si Puedes, and Chavez found work in a lumber mill. That year, Helen gave birth to their daughter Eloise.

Around that time, Father Donald McDonnell, a priest about Chavez's age, was introducing himself around Chavez's neighborhood. McDonnell fought for farmworkers' rights. As Chavez told historian Eugene Nelson, "I began going to the *bracero* camps with him to help with Mass, to the city jail with him to talk to prisoners, anything to be with him so that he could tell me more about the farm labor movement."

McDonnell encouraged Chavez to read about the cause. With his spotty education, Chavez couldn't read well. As he said years later, "I taught myself, and it unlocked a new world to me." Following McDonnell's advice, he read encyclicals (letters from Popes to other Catholics) that

Gandhi's Way

Chavez almost certainly read Mohandas Gandhi's *Non-Violence in Peace and War*. It was published in 1948, shortly before Chavez met Donald McDonnell. Here are a few quotes from Gandhi.

"Mental violence has no potency [power] and injures only the person whose thoughts are violent."

"The moment the slave resolves that he will no longer be a slave, his fetters fall."

"A non-violent revolution is not a program of seizure of power. It is a program of transformation of relationships, ending in a peaceful transfer of power."

supported labor unions. He also read books by Mohandas Gandhi, a leader who struggled to gain India's independence from Great Britain, that showed the power of nonviolent protest. Gandhi's ideas would guide Chavez for the rest of his life.

Something else stayed with Chavez too. A woman who attended McDonnell's services died, and Chavez helped move the body. The woman was heavy, and carrying her hurt Chavez's back. Forever after, his back would pain him.

At that time, white social scientists—college students and teachers who studied how people behave in groups—were going door to door, observing Latinos as if they were a separate species. As Chavez later told *The New Yorker* magazine, "They were interested in the worst barrio, the toughest slum, and they all picked Sal Si Puedes." One group after another came, asking personal questions about the Latinos' diet, sleeping arrangements, family lives, and other private matters. Afterwards, "They all go back and write their theses, and they never help people," said an observer named Fred Ross. When McDonnell recommended that Chavez meet Ross, Chavez thought that Ross was just another uncaring academic.

"I'VE FOUND THE GUY"

The gangly, modest Ross, fifteen years older than twenty-seven-year-old Chavez, had trained to be a teacher but had graduated during the depression and couldn't find a job. So he took work at the federal Farm Security Administration, giving food to poor people and helping to improve conditions in California farm laborers' camps.

After he left his government job, Ross worked for social-service organizations such as the Industrial Areas Foundation (IAF), a community-organizing group. When the IAF set up the Community Service Organization (CSO), a project that helped needy Latinos, Ross founded its Los Angeles chapter. Ross was so successful—in 1949, he helped elect Los Angeles's first Chicano city councilmember in almost seventy years—that by mid-1952, the CSO had him setting up other chapters throughout California.

When he reached San Jose, Ross asked McDonnell to name Mexican Americans who could become community leaders. One of McDonnell's nominees was Chavez.

Though he didn't trust Ross, Chavez was impressed that he seemed poor and sincere, and that he spoke some Spanish. Chavez arranged a "house meeting"—literally a meeting at the Chavez home with as many neighbors as he could fit—for June 9.

The Catholic Way

Father McDonnell encouraged Chavez to read Pope Leo XIII's *Encyclical on the Condition of Labor* (1891). These are a couple of quotes.

"A very few rich men and exceedingly rich men have laid a yoke almost of slavery on the unnumbered masses of non-owning workers."

"It is most clearly necessary that workers' associations . . . are being formed everywhere, and it is truly to be desired that they grow in number and in active vigor."

"[Ross] came in and sat down and began to talk about farmworkers, and then he took on the police and the politicians, not rabble-rousing either, but saying the truth," Chavez told journalist Peter Matthiessen. He was especially impressed when Ross mentioned that he and the CSO had fought for the rights of the Mexican American victims in the "Bloody Christmas" case.

Fred Ross would be a friend and ally of Chavez for the rest of his life.

Bloody Christmas

Christmas Day of 1951 brought pain and sadness for seven young Latinos. They had been arrested and were in their cells at Los Angeles's Lincoln Heights jail. In the hours before dawn, several Lincoln Heights police officers came to them. The cops had been having a Christmas party and were drunk. They beat the Latinos so savagely that blood streaked the walls and the prisoners nearly died.

"Bloody Christmas," as it was called, enraged Latinos nationwide. Los Angeles's Latino community called for an investigation and for greater civilian control over the police, as did groups of all races that fought for minorities' rights.

Eventually, the protests over Bloody Christmas got the guilty police officers fired. It was the first time that Los Angeles had punished its officers for abusing Mexican Americans.

Chavez asked Ross if the CSO would help the farmworkers create a union. "Fred told me, 'If CSO gets big enough, CSO will become a union,'" Chavez told writer Sam Kushner in the book *Long Road to Delano.* "So I said, 'Fine,' and I joined."

Ross saw Chavez's reaction differently. "No one there was more enthusiastic than Cesar," he told journalist John Gregory Dunne. "I was keeping a diary in those days, and that night when I got home, I wrote in it, 'I think I've found the guy I'm looking for.'"

THREE

Rising to the Top

Fred Ross was organizing a voter registration drive for 1952's November presidential elections. Chavez volunteered to help. At first, he had more will than skill. "When I knocked on the first door and a Chicano lady came out, I was so frightened I couldn't talk."

Still, he didn't quit. According to Ross, Chavez was the only person who went out each night for two solid months to get people to register to vote. He was earning Ross's admiration and becoming his friend.

Ross had to leave town to set up more CSO chapters, so he made Chavez the drive's chairperson. Chavez recruited friends to help. But, he told Peter Matthiessen, "Not one of them can qualify as a deputy registrar, not *one*. They can't even *vote*. Every damn one of these guys had a felony!" Still, they could talk to people, and they did.

After the registration drive signed up more than four thousand new voters, Ross hired Chavez to help him organize other CSO chapters full time. Once he was satisfied that Chavez could handle unfamiliar turf, Ross sent Chavez on his own to set up a chapter in Oakland, on the east side of San Francisco Bay.

OUT OF THE NEST

Chavez was scared to death. Unlike the sleepy agricultural towns that he knew, Oakland was filled with factories and was home to one of California's largest and busiest cargo-handling ports. And unlike other places where he'd lived, Oakland was crowded and bustling. While San Jose housed about 96,000 people over more than 171 square miles (443 square kilometers), Oakland packed four times as many people (385,000) into one-third as much space (less than 57 square miles [147 sq. km]).

On the way to house meetings, Chavez often got lost. When he got there, he circled the block over and over to get up the courage to enter. Once he entered, he was so shy that he could barely speak.

Eventually, though, he got the job done. Ross was so happy with his friend's work that in 1953, he gave Chavez the whole San Joaquin Valley

Chavez (right) worked diligently on the voter registration drive.

to organize. Chavez's new domain stretched across more than 15,000 square miles (about 40,000 sq. km)—more than two hundred times the size of Oakland.

To cover it all, Chavez became a migrant again. He dragged his entire family with him. It was becoming a very large group. In 1953, he and Helen had their fifth child, Anna. Organizing his vast territory kept him busy, and he had little time to spend with his children.

He was learning, though. When he faced harsh public criticism, he found that it could win him sympathy and new followers. When local CSO officers worried that working with Chavez could lose them their middle-class jobs, he discovered that some of his best officers were those with less to lose: working-class farmhands.

THE FIREBRAND

One of his best officers came his way in 1955. While Chavez was shy and not the arguing type, Dolores Huerta was an outspoken fighter. Like Fred Ross, the twenty-five-year-old Huerta had trained to be a teacher but longed to do something more important and went into social activism instead.

Ross found the tiny, fiery mother of two in 1955, when he arrived in the northern San Joaquin Valley town of Stockton for the CSO. "She had a reputation . . . as an especially dynamic woman who might have a future in politics," says *The Fight in the Fields*, by historians Susan Ferriss and Ricardo Sandoval. Huerta was helping to organize Catholic charities, but her tendency to speak out loudly and angrily against injustice marked her for more ambitious jobs. Ross took her into the CSO and assigned her to organize poor Latinos into political groups.

He also introduced her to Chavez. In the 1985 article "Reflections on the UFW Experience," Huerta remembered their first meeting. "He was a most self-effacing, soft-spoken person. . . . Five minutes after I met him, I couldn't find him again. He looked like everybody else. He was not the kind of person who called attention to himself. But he was a tremendously effective organizer." Chavez would eventually get over his shyness and would argue furiously with Huerta over tactics and strategy. Huerta, however, was as strong an ally as he could find.

OXNARD

Despite his traveling and long work hours, Chavez remained devoted to Helen. They had their sixth child, Paul, in 1957. The next one, Elizabeth, came along the next year, followed shortly by their final child, Anthony. As usual, Cesar left Helen to raise the children alone. He was working

The use of *braceros*, Mexican workers brought to the United States to work in the fields, made it difficult for farmworkers to negotiate for better pay and working conditions.

hard for the CSO and wanted to return to his original reason for joining the group: forming a farmworkers' union.

By 1958, he got close to it. Farmworkers in the Oxnard area already had an organization, the Packinghouse Workers Union (PWU), but local growers refused to hire its members. PWU president Ralph Helstein offered the CSO $20,000 if it would help the union. The CSO agreed and sent Chavez.

Chavez was eager to fight the growers but wasn't sure how. When he got to Oxnard in August 1958, he found that the problem was the farmworkers themselves. Specifically, it was the *braceros*.

The federal government allowed growers to use *braceros* only when there were no local workers, to hire them only for limited periods, and to pay them as much as local workers. In Oxnard and elsewhere, growers broke all of those rules.

Under Chavez's leadership, farmworkers and CSO members filed more than one thousand complaints with the state government. Chavez led the workers into the fields and staged protest marches. He also invited the press to witness and report these tactics.

The publicity caused the government to investigate Oxnard's growers. After Chavez revealed that government agencies were biased in the growers' favor, some of the most passionately pro-grower government officials lost their jobs.

In his memoirs, published in 1975, Chavez called the Oxnard project the most difficult of his entire career. Nevertheless, he was proud of the results. "This has been a wonderful experience," he wrote to Fred Ross when he left the assignment. "I never dreamed that so much hell could be raised."

GENERAL DIRECTING

Chavez was doing so well that in late 1958, the CSO promoted him to general director, one of the organization's highest positions. He stayed in Oxnard until late 1959, when the growers seemed ready to negotiate a contract. The PWU and the CSO's board of directors insisted that the union, not Chavez, do the negotiating. Frustrated, he left Oxnard for Los Angeles, the region's largest city and an appropriate place to set up headquarters.

He apparently spent his first year in Los Angeles getting to know people. Though Chavez was one of the few Latino leaders gaining prominence, others were making progress in their own ways.

Some of Chavez's fellow activists were involved with the "Viva Kennedy!" movement, which was a group of Latinos trying to elect Senator John F. Kennedy to the White House. Latino voters mattered enough that John's brother and campaign manager, Robert, met Chavez and asked him to help register Latino voters. The two men would become very important to each other.

Chavez encountered Reverend Wayne Hartmire, the head of the California Migrant Ministry, in 1961. The ministry tried to help migrant farmworkers. Chavez and Hartmire, nicknamed Chris, became friends. They would eventually team up to fight for the rights of workers.

Dolores Huerta, then CSO's lobbyist at the state capital in Sacramento, was another member of Chavez's team. In 1959, she worked with Donald McDonnell and others to set up the Agricultural Workers Organizing Committee. AWOC was part of the AFL-CIO, a huge organization made of two groups of unions, the American Federation of

Labor and the Congress of Industrial Organizations. AWOC waged a number of successful strikes, opposed the *bracero* system, and forced growers to raise farmworkers' pay.

Fighters

Chavez would become one of the most famous Latinos in the United States, but he wasn't the first to fight for Latino rights.

LULAC, the League of United Latin American Citizens, had been working since its founding in 1927 "to advance the economic condition, educational attainment, political influence, health and civil rights of the Hispanic population of the United States," according to the group's mission statement.

Since the 1930s, labor leader Bert Corona had been trying to organize poorly paid Latinos into a political and economic force and became a founder of UCAPAWA. In the 1940s, he fought to free Chicanos who had been unjustly arrested and jailed.

In 1954, Chicano attorney Gustavo "Gus" García won a landmark case, *Hernández* v. *Texas*, in which the Supreme Court decided that "persons of Mexican descent were systematically excluded from service" on juries. It was one of the first times that the Court recognized and outlawed discrimination against Latinos.

Victories like *Hernández* v. *Texas* were rare. In the late 1950s, most Latinos faced poverty, racism, and other injustices, and no large, widespread organization was doing much to help them. The United States would eventually see the growth of the Chicano movement, a rising tide of groups trying to make U.S. business, government, and society treat Latinos fairly. But at the time, it was only starting to stir.

By 1962, though, AWOC was faltering. The AFL-CIO's leaders were mostly industrial factory employees who didn't care much about farmworkers. Many AWOC leaders were white and didn't sign up Latino farmworkers. A few local AWOC chapters were strong, but they were filled with tight-knit groups of Filipino workers who didn't reach out to Latinos, either.

AWOC was so weak that in 1961, while on strike against the powerful lettuce grower Bud Antle, Inc., it didn't hinder Antle from signing a contract with the International Brotherhood of Teamsters. The Teamsters, a union composed of a variety of workers but best known as a freight handlers' union, broke the AWOC strike. They even let Bud Antle continue using *braceros*.

Meanwhile, Chavez still wanted to get into union organizing. He reached what Ross called "the turning point of his life." On March 31, 1962—his thirty-fifth birthday—Chavez proposed at a CSO meeting that the organization create its own farmworkers' union. The members, however, preferred concentrating on improving the lives of Latinos living in cities. When they voted Chavez down, he stood up. "I resign," he said.

Dolores Huerta fought alongside Chavez and sometimes against him.

FOUR

La Causa

T he room exploded. CSO members shouted at Chavez and at each other. Other members wept, including Dolores Huerta and Fred Ross.

In the future, when he discussed his resignation, Chavez often used the word "heartbroken." For ten years, the CSO had been his home. At that point, however, he planned to build a union. With Helen and the children, Chavez returned to Delano. His brother Richard was there, as was Helen's family. In Delano, said Chavez to writer John Gregory Dunne, "I would always have a roof over my head [and] a place to get a meal."

EFFORTS AND ALLIES

"For the next several months," Chavez told *The Nation* magazine journalist Ronald Taylor, "I went to the people. . . . I talked and I listened, trying to find out what they wanted." By the end of June, he had covered nearly 15,000 miles (24,135 km).

He also recruited help. On the Fourth of July, he contacted his cousin Manuel Chavez. Manuel was a successful car salesperson in San Diego and earned more than $18,000 per year at a time when the average person's income in the United States was less than $5,000. When Cesar asked him to join his cause, Manuel recalled in a contribution to Chavez's memoirs, he shouted, "You're crazy, man!" When Cesar reminded him of the uncaring and harsh treatment that they had received in the fields, though, Manuel promised to work with him.

Dolores Huerta was still working at the CSO, but she helped Chavez with his cause on weekends. Chavez's plans to start a union thrilled her, and she felt honored to be able to help out. By the end of the year, she quit her job at the CSO and joined Chavez's union full time.

Fred Ross helped as well. Because he was busy aiding Arizona's dirt-poor Yaqui Indians, he wasn't available all the time, but he performed a

Chavez poses with his wife and some of his children for a family portrait. He and his family returned to Delano to begin work on the union.

valuable service. When things got especially tough, Chavez would go to Ross and tell his troubles to him. Ross listened quietly and offered advice. The exchange made Chavez feel better and return with full strength to his work.

As the summer progressed, Chavez, Manuel, Huerta, and others asked farmworkers to send delegates to a meeting. In preparing for it, Cesar asked his brother Richard, who had some skill at design, to draw "an eagle of some type that shows strength, that shows power," as Richard told the authors of *The Fight in the Fields*. Richard based his design on the Aztec eagle that appears on the Mexican flag. Meanwhile, Cesar outlined his goals.

"WE'LL HAVE A UNION!"

In the heat of Sunday, September 30, about two hundred people gathered at a movie theater in the centrally located town of Fresno for the first

Some attendees of the first National Farm Workers Association convention gather for a photograph. In the background is the NFWA motto: "Viva La Causa."

National Farm Workers Association (NFWA) convention. Chavez read his list of goals. While most farmworkers earned $1.00 or less per hour, NFWA would fight for a minimum hourly wage of $1.50. It would also fight to get the workers life insurance and unemployment insurance, and would set up a credit union so the members could borrow money.

Brown paper covered the theater's movie screen. On Chavez's cue, Manuel ripped the paper away to reveal an enormous flag that he'd made from Richard's design. The black, angular eagle hovered in a white circle on a field of bold red.

To some delegates, the design looked disturbingly like the Nazi flag. Chavez and Manuel talked them into accepting it, with Manuel declaring, "When that damn eagle flies, we'll have a union!" The members also endorsed a proposed motto: "*Viva La Causa!*" meaning "Long Live the Cause!"

La Causa and *La Raza*

La Causa meant different things to different people. To many activists living in cities and college campuses, *La Causa* meant improving the lives of all Latinos. These activists were concerned with what they called *La Raza*—the Hispanic race. To them, Chavez was a hero. To Chavez, though, *La Causa* was more important than *La Raza*. He focused on farmworkers, even the ones who weren't Latino. While he was proud to be Latino and occasionally seemed to favor Latinos over other members of his union, he would get angry at activists who expected him to focus solely on *La Raza*. "Why be racist?" he asked one activist group. "Our belief is to help everyone, not just one race."

BUILDING AND GROWING

Over the next three years, Chavez and his allies spread the NFWA gospel. By day, Chavez worked the fields with Helen and their older children, earning a tiny income by picking cotton and other crops. By night, he devoted himself to setting up the union. The work devoured his savings and income, and he sometimes had to borrow food from sympathetic supporters, but he was getting things done.

Chavez planned the union's constitution and structure, talked to insurance companies about setting up an insurance plan for union members, and founded the NFWA credit union to provide loans to members. At the same time, he encouraged workers to join the NFWA. "By 1964," says *Cesar Chavez: A Triumph of Spirit* by Richard Griswold del Castillo and Richard A. Garcia, "the association had 1,000 dues-paying members and more than 50 local [chapter]s. They opened a union office in Delano . . . built with donations of labor and materials from throughout the San Joaquin Valley."

Chavez didn't stop there. In 1964, he founded the union newspaper *El Malcriado*. The name, which is difficult to translate exactly, means roughly "the ill-bred" or "the brat." The newspaper dubbed itself "The Voice of the Farm Worker" and was useful in spreading the union's view of its struggles.

Chavez struck a little luck when the U.S. Congress decided that the *bracero* program would end on December 31, 1964. Some growers would still bring in cheap, temporary workers, but the federal government no longer encouraged the practice. One of the greatest obstacles to a farmworkers' union was disappearing.

Some of NFWA's more passionate members wanted to stage strikes or walkouts immediately. Not Chavez. "I thought it would be four years, maybe five, before we'd be ready for a strike," he told labor journalist Dick Meister, "and I was really scared we might go too soon and get crushed."

FIRST STRIKES

In the spring of 1965, rose grafter Epifanio Camacho left the fields a few miles south of Delano and went to see Chavez. The growers had promised the grafters $9.00 for every one thousand plants that they grafted, but they actually paid between $6.50 and $7.00. Camacho and other rose workers wanted to go on strike and wanted NFWA's help.

Chavez tried to talk them out of striking, but they were determined to go ahead. The grafters authorized NFWA to negotiate with the growers and promised not to return to work until the dispute was resolved. Four days later, the growers raised the grafters' wages. NFWA had won its first strike.

Almost 250 miles (400 km) south of Delano, in the Coachella Valley north of Mexico, AWOC grape pickers were furious. The AWOC workers, who were mostly of Filipino ancestry, earned $1.25 an hour while Department of Labor rules granted workers from Mexico $1.40 per hour. In May of 1965, AWOC pickers went on strike. Within days, the growers agreed to pay them as much as they paid the Mexicans.

In Delano, AWOC grape pickers faced the same problem and made the same demands, but Delano's growers wouldn't pay up. On September 8, AWOC leader Larry Itliong led more than one thousand of his union's workers in walking off the job. Like the rose grafters, they asked NFWA for help.

The young union was still weak and didn't have much money. "All I could think was, 'Oh, God, we're not ready for a strike,'" Chavez told John Gregory Dunne.

Other NFWA members disagreed. Under pressure, Chavez called a strike vote. On the night of September 16—Mexican Independence Day—at least five hundred farmworkers and their families crammed into Delano's Our Lady of Guadalupe Catholic Church.

Chavez gave a speech, saying that the union's members "are engaged in [a] struggle for the freedom and dignity which poverty denies us. But it must not be a violent struggle." He added, "The strike was begun by Filipinos, but it is not exclusively for them. Tonight, we must decide if we are to join our fellow workers."

The vote was virtually unanimous. They would strike. According to Eugene Nelson, "'*Que viva la huelga!* Long live the strike!' And '*Viva!*,' the whole auditorium erupts in chorus. . . . The cheers continue for a good ten minutes. . . . '*Viva la causa! Viva Cesar Chavez! Viva la union!*'"

NFWA members and AWOC members picket a grape grower's farm and delay one of its trucks from leaving.

FIVE

Picketing, Boycotting, and Marching

NFWA began participating officially in AWOC's grape strike on Monday, September 20, 1965. Starting before dawn, hundreds of NFWA members marched alongside AWOC members while brandishing signs carrying the NFWA eagle and the word HUELGA (strike).

Grape harvesting season has traditionally been short, lasting usually just two months per year. If the growers couldn't get someone to pick grapes by the end of October, they would lose a year's worth of profit. On the other hand, the strikers had very little money, and most of them earned nothing while on strike. They, too, wanted to settle the strike quickly.

With pressure on both workers and growers, things quickly got ugly. While visiting the picket lines and working in NFWA's tiny, crowded Delano office, Chavez heard that growers and their ranch foremen were grabbing picket signs and shooting them to bits, pointing shotguns at the protesters, beating them bloody, spraying them with deadly insecticides, and driving cars and trucks at them. What's more, the police followed, photographed, and interrogated the picketers.

Nevertheless, the union pressed on, and the strike spread. "By early October, dozens of table-grape operations in the southern San Joaquin Valley were being struck by about 3,000 farmworkers," wrote Patrick Mooney and Theo Majka in *Farmers' and Farm Workers' Movements: Social Protest in American Agriculture.*

ENTERTAINMENT WITH A PUNCH

Chavez and the striking workers received help from several sources. Luis Valdez, the son of Delano-area farmworkers, had recently graduated from San Jose State University with a degree in theater. He returned to Delano, eager to help the farmworkers, and asked Chavez for permission to put on shows for them. When Chavez said yes, Valdez gathered a group of performers and named them El Teatro Campesino (The Peasant Theater).

The actors took shows to the workers, traveling to lines of picketers in a flatbed truck that they used as their stage. Most of the actors had been farmworkers at some point, and their shows reflected what they knew and felt. Under Valdez's direction, the performers sang and put on *actos*, playlets that made fun of the union's enemies. "All the skits . . . reached predictably uplifting climaxes—a scab [strikebreaker] was converted, a grape grower got his come-uppance," *The New Yorker* magazine reported, "but they all made their points through good, wholesome, frequently amusing slapstick."

Artists in other fields also helped get the message across. Illustrators created posters and cartoons, while musicians wrote and performed *corridos* (story-telling ballads) about the farmworkers' struggles and dreams.

THE BERKELEY INCIDENT

On October 19, 1965, during a fund-raising tour of northern California colleges, Chavez was speaking to a huge crowd at the University of California at Berkeley. Suddenly, NFWA volunteer Wendy Goepel handed him a slip of paper. He told the students, "I have just received a telegram informing me that forty-four of our pickets have been arrested for yelling '*Huelga*.'"

It was true. Two days earlier, Sergeant Gerald Dodd of the Kern County sheriff's department had arrested an NFWA ally, the Migrant Ministry's Reverend David Havens, for disturbing the peace by reading novelist Jack London's angry "Definition of a Strikebreaker" aloud on a Delano street. Chavez and his partners made plans to fight this assault on their freedom to protest.

On October 19, the picketers arrived at the W. B. Camp Ranch, southeast of Delano. Among them were Chris Hartmire and eight other ministers, plus Helen Chavez. Word of their plans had gotten out; reporters were watching, as were Sergeant Dodd and other police officers. The picketers called out to the strikebreakers in the fields. As Chavez had expected, the officers arrested them.

In Berkeley, the students yelled "*Huelga! Huelga!*" On Chavez's request, they gave him the money they would have spent on lunch: about $2,000. By the time he finished touring the area's campuses,

Picking at Scabs

"**D**efinition of a Strikebreaker," the Jack London essay that Havens read, became central to Chavez's efforts and appeared on the walls of NFWA offices. A strikebreaker, also called a scab, is someone who works in a field or factory even if its union has staged a walkout, but London's definition is more vivid than that.

After God had finished the rattlesnake, the toad [and] the vampire, He had some awful substance left with which He made a scab. A scab is a two-legged animal with a corkscrew soul, a water-logged brain, and a combination backbone made of jelly and glue. Where others have hearts, he carries a tumor of rotten principle.

When a scab comes down the street, men turn their backs, and angels weep in Heaven, and the devil shuts the gates of Hell to keep him out. No man has a right to scab so long as there is a pool of water to drown his body in, or a rope long enough to hang his carcass with.

Judas Iscariot was a gentleman compared with a scab. For betraying his Master, he had character enough to hang himself—a scab has not. Esau sold his birthright for a mess of pottage. Judas Iscariot sold his Savior for 30 pieces of silver. Benedict Arnold sold his country for the promise of a commission in the British Army.

The modern strikebreaker sells his birthright, his country, his wife, his children, and his fellow man for an unfilled promise from his employer, trust, or corporation. Esau was a traitor to himself. Judas Iscariot was a traitor to his God. Benedict Arnold was a traitor to his country; a strikebreaker to his God, his country, his family, his class.

A real man will never scab.

he took back more than $6,000, plus vast publicity and streams of volunteers.

As 1965 approached its end, things started to look better. The forty-four jailed protesters were set free. Members of the Teamsters Union and the International Longshoremen's and Warehousemen's Union supported NFWA by refusing to load San Joaquin Valley grapes onto ships at the San Francisco pier. An anonymous donor gave NFWA the Forty Acres, an empty field where the union would build its new headquarters.

Yet the growers still refused to negotiate a contract.

THE IRISH STRATEGY

Chavez turned to a boycott. Irish leader Charles Parnell had developed the technique in the 1880s to protest high rents that landowners such as the Earl of Erne charged their tenants. Parnell encouraged the tenants to fight the earl's hired landlord, Charles Boycott, "by leaving him severely alone!" From then on, no one did business with Boycott.

In mid-December, Chavez launched a boycott against Schenley Industries, a major San Joaquin Valley winemaker. His timing was perfect.

When Chavez started the Schenley boycott, the AFL-CIO was holding a convention in San Francisco, about 200 miles (less than 350 km) northwest of Delano. Paul Schrade, a young official of the AFL-CIO's powerful United Auto Workers union, sympathized with the NFWA. He talked the UAW's nationally famous president, Walter Reuther, into joining Chavez and local AWOC chief Larry Itliong on a December 16 march through Delano.

Reuther loved it. The grape strike reminded him of the 1930s, when UAW strikes improved conditions for auto workers. He proudly held a HUELGA sign, told the farmworkers, "This is not *your* strike; this is *our* strike!", and promised the strikers $5,000 a month. Moreover, he brought the strike national attention. Still, the growers wouldn't negotiate. Chavez needed a new tactic. He considered a protest march but wasn't sure where it should go.

In February of 1966, consumer advocate William Bennett, a California Public Utilities Commission member and an ally of Chavez's, pointed out that the state government was contributing to the farmworkers' troubles. The legislature refused to guarantee farmworkers a minimum wage, thereby dooming them to endless poverty. At the same time, however, it guaranteed a high price for Schenley wines. That was all Chavez had to hear. The march would head to the state capital, Sacramento.

Chavez and his allies planned the pilgrimage for mid-March. Again, his timing was perfect. On March 16, Senators Harrison Williams,

Walter Reuther (center) shows his support by accompanying Chavez (right) on a march through Delano.

George Murphy, and Robert Kennedy of the Senate Subcommittee on Migratory Labor conducted hearings in Delano's high school auditorium. The hearings brought even more attention to Chavez's movement. Chavez testified, "All we want from the government is the machinery—some rules of the game. All we need is the recognition of our right to full and equal coverage under every law which protects every other working man and woman."

Kennedy endorsed the NFWA's strike and boycott, the first national politician to do so. While Reuther's visit brought Chavez attention, Kennedy's popularity among liberal-minded Americans brought support. People nationwide, especially in large cities, stopped buying Schenley wines.

PILGRIMAGE

On March 17, the day after the hearings, Chavez and his crew—estimates range from sixty-eight people to about one hundred—started a pilgrimage of more than 200 miles (more than 300 km) north to Sacramento. They waved flags,

Chavez testifies about the farmworkers' situation during a Senate Subcommittee on Migratory Labor hearing.

HUELGA signs, and images of the Virgin Mary of Guadalupe, Mexico's matron saint.

Virgin Power

Some union marchers who weren't observant Mexican Catholics grumbled about traveling under the sign of the Virgin. But Chavez knew that the symbol had power, especially among Mexicans and Mexican Americans.

The Virgin's story started in 1531, a decade after Spanish conquistadors had overrun Mexico. A vision of a teenage, brown-skinned Virgin Mary appeared to a humble Mexican Indian named Juan Diego on a hill named Tepeyac, where an Aztec temple had once stood. The Virgin told Diego to build a chapel there, but when Diego tried to tell the bishop of his church about his vision, the bishop wouldn't listen. To convince the bishop, the story goes, the Virgin made an image of herself appear on Juan Diego's cloak.

From then on, the Virgin Mary of Guadalupe became a hero to people of Mexican descent. Her story meant that a divine power cared about everyone, even people whom the world scorned. In 1810, her image decorated the banner of Father Miguel Hidalgo when he declared Mexico's independence from Spain. A century later, popular Mexican leaders Pancho Villa and Emiliano Zapata rode under the Virgin's flag. When Pope John Paul II visited Mexico in 1979, he said, "Wherever there is a Mexican, there is the Mother of Guadalupe. Someone recently told me that 96 out of 100 Mexicans are Catholic, but 100 out of 100 are Guadalupeans!"

Within Chavez's union, the Virgin had a special place. "She is a symbol of faith, hope, and leadership," Dolores Huerta said. "She is strength, and she is beauty, and she is wisdom and compassion."

The pilgrimage wasn't easy, especially at first. Chavez's back ached and forced him to limp. Soon, blisters covered his feet. He even ran a fever.

Still, spirits were high. "All through the little towns in the heart of the Central Valley, we marched—singing union songs and workers' songs and songs for joy," Chavez said in an article in *Look* magazine. *The Fight in the Fields* adds, "As the walkers approached each new town, their ranks would swell." On April 5, in Stockton, the number grew to five thousand marchers.

That night, Chavez got a phone call from Sidney Korshak, Schenley's lawyer for labor affairs. A large union involved with delivering alcohol from warehouses to customers—some sources say the Teamsters, others say the Bartenders Association—was apparently refusing to handle Schenley wines. The refusal and the consumer boycott were too much for Schenley's owners, who told Korshak to settle the strike.

VICTORY

Overnight, Chris Hartmire drove Chavez some 350 miles (550 km) south to Korshak's Beverly Hills estate. Chavez and Korshak agreed that

As the protesters made their way to Sacramento, more and more people came out to show their support for Chavez and the cause.

This was
one of many
demonstrations
against Schenley.

Schenley would hire farmworkers through an NFWA hiring hall (a job-placement office) and raise their wages by 35 cents an hour. "Not counting Hawaii, where the International Longshoremen's and Warehousemen's Union had won contracts for pineapple workers, it was the first such contract ever negotiated in the history of American farm labor," John Gregory Dunne wrote. Chavez rejoined the pilgrimage in triumph.

On April 10, Easter Sunday, the pilgrims hit Sacramento like an army liberating an oppressed village. More than three thousand supporters came to walk with them. At least five thousand more met them by the state capitol's steps. The march showed the power of Chavez's leadership.

That summer, NFWA merged with AWOC into the AFL-CIO United Farmworkers Organizing Committee (UFWOC), with Chavez as president and Larry Itliong as vice president. "That was a survival decision," Dolores Huerta wrote in 1985. "Had we not merged, the Teamsters Union would have wiped us out, because they moved into the fields in 1966." In particular, they moved into DiGiorgio's fields.

California's largest fruit grower, the DiGiorgio Corporation farmed more than 4,400 acres (nearly 1,800 ha) at Delano, and much more elsewhere. Its products included the nationally famous TreeSweet juices and S&W canned foods. It earned more than $200 million a year. "The company was linked to the state's major financial, industrial, retail, and real-estate institutions," wrote John Gregory Dunne. And it hated unions. "DiGiorgio had broken every farm labor strike against it."

ELECTION

Like Bud Antle in 1961, DiGiorgio wanted to use the Teamsters to keep a competing union out of its fields. DiGiorgio's workers would elect either UFWOC or the Teamsters. If UFWOC lost, other growers would invite the Teamsters in, and Chavez's union would likely die.

DiGiorgio fought dirty. After announcing that it would allow an election, the company promptly fired 190 workers, apparently to keep them from voting for UFWOC. Chavez, Fred Ross, and others went into DiGiorgio's fields, spending hours trying to convince workers to choose their union.

On August 30, 1966, the workers voted. The next morning, the word came in: UFWOC had won. Stunned and saddened by the verdict, Delano's merchants closed their stores for the rest of the day. But at Filipino Hall, a local assembly room where union members had gathered, word of UFWOC's victory triggered celebrations. Unionists cheered and sang in joy until Chavez said, "Okay, we've won, but we can't sit on our laurels. Let's go get another one." After an early lunch, they returned to picketing at a nearby ranch.

The Teamsters fought back. The country's biggest union, with literally millions of members, worked persistently to sign contracts with growers and keep UFWOC out. The Teamsters didn't have Chavez's staying power, though. After one particularly drawn-out battle—an eleven-month fight over the Perelli-Minetti Winery about 45 miles (72 km) southeast of Delano—the Teamsters had apparently had enough. In July 1967, the two unions signed an agreement not to compete for the same workers. Little UFWOC had beaten the biggest bully in organized labor.

Chavez and other members of the UFWOC celebrate their victory over the Teamsters.

More, Bigger, and Bloodier

As Chavez signed up more wineries, he was becoming a star. Journalists wrote articles about him, people who sympathized with farmworkers praised him, and people who sympathized with growers criticized him. New supporters came his way. Feisty liberal attorney Jerry Cohen, for instance, joined Chavez in 1967 as UFWOC's lawyer.

Others took his side as well. The California Migrant Ministry and the Catholic Bishops of California supported Chavez and the UFWOC. Prominent politicians, particularly Democrats, spoke up for the boycott. Chavez was especially a hero to Chicanos. Until he came along, no Mexican American had achieved national prominence and large-scale success in leading a fight for their rights. His appeal spread far beyond the poor farmworkers whom he defended. "Only Chavez had the reputation and support that crossed class and generational as well as regional lines," says *Cesar Chavez: A Triumph of Spirit.* Images of Chavez appeared on murals and posters in communities with sizable Latino populations. Latino political organizations courted his support. Even some non-Latino politicians grew interested in his endorsement because they knew that his popularity among Latino voters could help them win elections.

Still, Chavez's main business was running UFWOC. He branched out, dispatching union officials to organize farmworkers in Florida, Arizona, and Texas. He spoke out against the use of dangerous agricultural pesticides, unfair immigration laws, and other topics only slightly related to the fight for better working conditions.

FAMILY MATTERS

As times got tough, Chavez leaned on his wife, Helen. According to *The Fight in the Fields*, their son Paul found a notebook of his father's dated spring 1967. One entry read, "It's very tough. I don't know if I can continue." Two days later, another entry declared, "I spoke to Helen. I'm ready to go."

Helen gave Cesar more than emotional support. She ran UFWOC's credit union and raised their eight children. "It's lucky I have Helen there because I'm never really home. . . . Sometimes I'm away for 10 nights, maybe more," Chavez told Peter Matthiessen in 1968. "I never once took [my oldest son] fishing or to a ball game."

"It hurts me not to be home with my family," Chavez added. "But what about the work that has to be done?" UFWOC, after all, was still a small union. Only about 5,000 of California's 250,000 farmworkers belonged to it. The union had won the right to negotiate with only a few growers and had signed contracts with even fewer.

Tired of going after one grower at a time, Chavez wanted to fight and win a battle large enough to pull whole groups of growers into line. In the summer of 1967, UFWOC targeted Giumarra Vineyards, California's largest grower of table grapes—that is, grapes to be eaten rather than made into wine. Like the Half Moon Bay pea farm that Chavez had worked in 1938, Giumarra paid ordinary piecework rates but counted only the best pickings toward payments. The result was low wages for its workers.

Giumarra was wily. When UFWOC convinced its workers to go on strike in early August, Giumarra got a court order to stop them. When Chavez called on consumers to stop buying Giumarra grapes, the company shipped grapes under other growers' labels. So in January of 1968, UFWOC announced a boycott of all California table grapes.

Though the boycott soon hurt growers, the union was hurting as well. UFWOC was splitting into factions. Latino members complained

Chavez stands with a group of striking union members in 1967.

that Chavez surrounded himself with too many whites. Radical leftists felt that the union was too moderate. Members who weren't religious were uncomfortable with the union's Catholic leanings. Even members who hated the growers were dangerous, as far as Chavez was concerned, because he wanted to sign contracts with the growers. In several speeches, Chavez told those members, "If you think that all growers are [rotten], you're no good to us."

The members didn't always listen. As the strike and boycott dragged on for months without squeezing anything from the growers, union radicals pushed for anti-grower violence. The radicals noted that other groups with goals like UFWOC's were using violence, or at least threatening it. Furious about the United States's war in Vietnam and other crises, these groups spoke about bringing on a revolution. Students for a Democratic Society, a nationwide group dedicated to creating antipoverty programs and attaining equal rights for all races, was developing factions that advocated terrorist acts to bring down the government. Meanwhile, the Black Panther Party called on African Americans to own guns and practice armed self-defense to protect themselves from the police.

Besides, argued UFWOC's radical members, the growers had used violence against the union members. Among other tactics, they drove trucks at lines of picketing workers to make them disperse. Near Delano in October of 1966, Lowell Schy, a grower's sales representative, ran down picketer Manuel Rivera and permanently crippled him. That same month, a deputy sheriff in Starr County, Texas, hit a union organizer and held a gun to his forehead for shouting "*viva la huelga*" while under arrest in the county courthouse. In May of the next year, members of the Texas

Rangers, a group of state-sponsored law officers, arrested union supporters Magdaleno Dimas and Reverend Edgar Krueger, roughed them up, and held their faces just inches from a train that was barreling by.

Similar assaults took place wherever UFWOC went. The radicals wanted to fight back, but Chavez didn't. "If we had used violence, we would have won contracts long ago," Chavez admitted to Matthiessen, "but they wouldn't be lasting, because we wouldn't have won respect."

That kind of sentiment didn't slow down the radicals. Chavez needed to stop the their headlong rush to violence, hold their attention until their passions cooled down, and divert their minds toward his principles. To accomplish this aim, he stopped eating.

GOING HUNGRY

The inspiration for Chavez's fast came from his hero, Mohandas Gandhi. Time after time in the 1920s, Gandhi's followers turned to violence. To shock them into stopping, Gandhi fasted, sometimes for weeks at a time. As he said in 1924, "A son can fast against a father addicted to drink to cure him of his evil. The father knows it to be evil and realizes the enormity of it by the sufferings of his son, and he corrects himself. . . . My fasting brought home to [my followers] their mistake, and they corrected it."

Chavez hoped that his own fast would have the same effect. His last full day of eating was February 13, 1968, after he had finished a national fund-raising tour. "I don't like the whole idea. I think it's ridiculous," said Helen. She tried to tempt him out of it by preparing his favorite foods, such as chopped chicken liver and spicy East Indian dishes. However, Chavez wouldn't bite.

When he called a union meeting to tell the members about the fast, they didn't like it any more than Helen did. They wept and shouted as the CSO members had when Chavez resigned.

To shield his family from any unwanted attention that the fast would attract, Chavez moved into the Forty Acres. At first, he suffered from hunger pains and headaches. After a week, the pain subsided, and he wasn't even hungry anymore. But as the days passed, the pain returned—this time, in his legs, back, and joints.

Farmworkers, UFWOC volunteers, and others pitched tents on the Forty Acres, apparently to support Chavez as he fasted. To show their allegiance, they raised crucifixes, UFWOC flags, and pictures of the Virgin Mary of Guadalupe.

Near the end of February, the still-fasting Chavez went to Bakersfield, the region's largest city, to face a contempt-of-court charge connected to Giumarra Vineyards' court order against striking. "Thousands of farmworkers appeared and filled the courthouse beyond its capacity," says *Cesar Chavez: A Triumph of Spirit.* "The media coverage of the event was invaluable in publicizing the boycott." Chavez eventually won the case.

Returning to the Forty Acres, Chavez continued fasting. He received messages of support from politicians such as Robert Kennedy and activists such as Martin Luther King, Jr. Chavez's friends, family, and doctors kept pressuring him to eat.

Finally, on March 10, thousands of people gathered at a Delano park to watch Robert Kennedy give Chavez—too weak to stand or speak—a piece of bread, his first food in more than three weeks. The fast was over.

For the fast's end, Chavez had written a speech. Because he was too frail to read it aloud, he had Reverend James Drake, a friend and ally, read it. The speech's last lines became famous: "I am convinced that the truest act of courage, the strongest act of manliness, is to sacrifice ourselves for others in a totally nonviolent struggle for justice. To be a man is to suffer for others. God help us to be men!"

Activists of the 1960s

During the middle and late 1960s, several leaders fought problems similar to the ones that Chavez was battling. Reverend Martin Luther King, Jr. spoke out against racism and demanded equality for African Americans. Like Chavez, he advocated nonviolence even when some of his colleagues disagreed. He endured jailings and other pressures to make him stop his activities. Nothing silenced King until an assassin's bullet killed him on April 4, 1968.

In 1963, journalist Betty Friedan published *The Feminine Mystique*, a book exposing discrimination against women. In June of 1966, she and other women gathered to form NOW, the National Organization for Women. Friedan and her colleagues worked to get women the rights and freedoms that men enjoyed.

While King was in his late thirties during the mid-1960s and Friedan was in her early forties, activists Abbie Hoffman, Tom Hayden, and Jerry Rubin were a decade younger. They led mass demonstrations of other young men and women on college campuses and elsewhere to protest the United States's involvement in the Vietnam War, among other causes. At one set of demonstrations during the Democratic Party's national convention in July of 1968, the police brutally attacked the demonstrators. The nationally televised violence became a symbol of the furious divisions among citizens of the United States at that time.

As Chavez had hoped, his fast dampened the threat of violence and united UFWOC's members. A week later, Robert Kennedy put that unity to use. Through one of his allies, Paul Schrade, he asked union members to support him as a candidate for president. The union agreed and set up voter-registration drives in Latino areas.

UFWOC's efforts succeeded spectacularly. "Some precincts in East Los Angeles had, for the first time in their history, a 100% voter turnout," says *Cesar Chavez: A Triumph of Spirit.* "Almost all voted for Kennedy."

Kennedy won in California. On June 4, election night, Chavez, Schrade, Dolores Huerta, and hundreds of other Kennedy supporters celebrated at Los Angeles's Ambassador Hotel. When the crowd began shouting Chavez's name, he felt embarrassed and left, but Huerta and Schrade stayed behind. As Kennedy gave his victory speech, they stood with him. A few minutes later, they were walking behind him when assassin Sirhan Sirhan shot him to death.

"It was so senseless!" Chavez wrote in his memoirs. He was at a party for Latino politician Richard Calderon when he heard the news. The next day, he returned to Delano.

Robert Kennedy shows his support for Cesar Chavez, helping him break his fast and bringing the media spotlight on Chavez's work.

After Kennedy's assassination, Chavez started traveling with body-guards. He also adopted two black shepherd dogs, Boycott and Huelga. He loved the dogs. At one point, he even said that if he weren't a labor leader, he might like to be a dog trainer.

NEW AGONIES

In the fall of 1968, Chavez was hospitalized with back pain that immobilized him. The pain was so severe that he wanted to die. The doctors couldn't identify the pain's source, and Chavez left the hospital and returned to his office, flat on his back and gaunt from weight loss.

By early 1969, when his agonies were at their worst, the DiGiorgio Corporation had quietly sold its farms. The new owners ignored DiGiorgio's UFWOC contract. The gains that the union had made in 1966 were gone.

In January of 1969, Richard Nixon became president. During his election campaign, Nixon had shown contempt for UFWOC by calling its boycott illegal and publicly eating California grapes. As president, he ordered the Department of Defense to defy the boycott and nearly double its order of grapes for the military, from 6.9 to 11 million pounds (3.1 to 4.9 million kilograms). The governor of California, Ronald Reagan, also opposed the boycott and publicly announced that he ate plenty of grapes.

At that point the longest agricultural walkout in U.S. history, the strike dragged on with few results. The slow, endless struggle depressed the union's members and even its leaders.

Luckily for Chavez, the boycott was taking hold. From late 1967 to the start of 1969, grape sales fell by 10 percent to 25 percent, depending on who was counting. In January of 1969, the California Department of Health gave consumers an extra reason to boycott the grapes by reporting that pesticides were poisoning farmworkers.

The next month, back doctor Janet Travell arrived. Years earlier, when John Kennedy had had back problems, Travell had treated them. At the request of UFWOC nurse Marion Moses and Kennedy connection Paul Schrade, Travell went to Delano. She found that one of Chavez's legs was shorter than the other. In adjusting his movements to compensate, he was unknowingly pinching muscles in his back.

After Travell gave him painkillers and showed him ways to sit and move, Chavez's pain began to subside. He would never be completely without pain, but he returned gradually to public life.

BACK TO BOYCOTTING

On May 10, 1969, Chavez was feeling well enough to launch two new projects. One was a "secondary boycott," in which consumers not only refused to buy California grapes but also refused to buy anything in stores that sold them. On the same day, to publicize the boycott, Chavez led a 100-mile (160-km) march from the date-growing Coachella Valley town of Indio to Calexico on the Mexican border. When the march ended on May 18, hundreds of farmworkers and Senators Walter Mondale and Edward Kennedy (Robert's brother) were there to cheer.

Coachella Valley grape grower Lionel Steinberg was probably paying attention. A liberal Democrat, he had for months been trying to lead growers to negotiate with Chavez. On June 20, negotiations began.

For a long time, the negotiations didn't go anywhere. But Chavez did. In July, his face graced *Time* magazine's cover, proving that he had become an important national figure. In August, he traveled to Washington, D.C., and denounced the use of pesticides in hearings before Congress, in protests at the federal Food and Drug Administration, and in public statements. "Pesticide poisoning," he declared, "is more important today than even wages." In September, he traveled east again, spending several weeks in Michigan, Ohio, Pennsylvania, New York, Ontario, Massachusetts, and other areas to promote UFWOC's goals. He met mayors, senators, union leaders, and Catholic bishops, and journalists interviewed him on national television. In January of 1970, Steven Roberts, the *New York Times's* chief reporter in southern California, wrote, "Cesar Chavez has become the nation's favorite radical."

The boycott spread, but growers wouldn't sign new contracts. At the start of April 1970, *U.S. News & World Report* magazine published a story

titled "Whatever Happened to . . . the Grape Strike and Boycott." The answer wasn't long in coming.

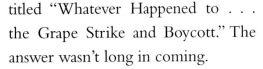

Chavez's efforts on behalf of the union were drawing a lot of attention. He appeared on the July 4 issue of *Time* magazine, a national news publication.

More consumers began to buy grapes with the union label, which put pressure on the growers to negotiate with the UFWOC.

SEVEN

Endings and Beginnings

In early April 1970, after nearly a year of negotiating, Lionel Steinberg became the first grower to sign a UFWOC contract since 1967. "The contract calls for $1.75 an hour plus 25¢ for each box of grapes picked, in contrast to the current rate of $1.65 an hour and 15¢ a box," said the *San Francisco Chronicle*. "In addition, [Steinberg] will put 10¢ an hour into a health and welfare fund and two cents into an economic development fund to help workers who lose their jobs because of old age or mechanization [replacing workers with machines]. The contract also sets up a hiring hall run by the union and provides safeguards in the use of pesticides."

Steinberg was delighted to find major chain grocery stores calling him to purchase his union-approved grapes. Because the stores would buy from him and not from the growers still being boycotted, he found himself outselling the other growers.

The other growers noticed. One by one over the spring and summer of 1970, they signed union contracts. Like Steinberg, they saw their sales increase. After years of holding the union in contempt, growers—up to fifty a week—started calling UFWOC to ask, "What do I have to do to get the bird [the union's black eagle] on my grapes?"

Not everyone signed, though. Delano's growers had always fought hardest against Chavez, and they refused to give in. Chavez was working on ways to make them give in when he got an emergency call from an ally in Salinas, a lettuce-growing town about 150 miles (240 km) northwest of Delano.

BACK AND FORTH

In the late spring and early summer of 1970, UFWOC had been working to sign up farmworkers in the Salinas area and in the lettuce fields near Santa Maria, about 150 miles (240 km) down the coast. Lettuce growers worried that UFWOC would squeeze them as it was squeezing the grape growers.

The lettuce growers were negotiating new contracts for truck drivers with Bill Grami, the Teamsters' shrewd, ambitious executive for farmworkers. On July 23, the growers decided to have Grami deploy the Teamsters to keep UFWOC from signing up their workers. The move meant breaking UFWOC's 1967 "no competition" pact with the Teamsters, but Grami didn't care. "UFWOC had 'flagrantly violated' the peace treaty by striking, Grami reasoned, so he was free to begin organizing field workers again," says *A Long Time Coming*, a history of farm labor.

On July 24, an ally in Salinas placed an emergency call to Chavez, saying that the Teamsters had entered the lettuce fields. They were telling the workers that the growers planned to sign Teamster contracts, and adding that if the workers wanted to keep their jobs, they had better join the Teamsters union.

If the Teamsters won, Chavez felt, his union would collapse. He drove up to Salinas to look into the situation and rally the workers. When he got back late on the night of July 25, Chavez wanted only to rest, but UFWOC lawyer Jerry Cohen had called. Giumarra, the large grape grower, had changed its mind and wanted to finish negotiating right away.

If Giumarra signed a contract with UFWOC, other Delano growers would sign contracts too. For the next few days, negotiations went on constantly.

As Chavez and his team edged close to victory, the lettuce growers announced that they had signed contracts with the Teamsters. Chavez raced to Salinas for a press conference and meetings with workers to plan walkouts and a protest march, and then hurried back to Delano.

On July 29, a group of more than two dozen grape growers, including Giumarra and the growers who had bought out DiGiorgio, signed up with Chavez's union. The hiring hall that UFWOC had wanted, a promise of protection from pesticides, a wage of $1.80 an hour with a

Two former adversaries, Cesar Chavez and John Giumarra, Jr., shake hands and announce a new contract between Giumarra and UFWOC.

raise in 1972 to $2.05, an additional payment of 10 cents an hour per worker for the union's Robert F. Kennedy Health and Welfare Fund to benefit sick or disabled workers, a payment of 2 cents per box for the union's economic development fund—Chavez got it all. No one in U.S. agricultural history had ever scored such a victory.

When UFWOC and the AFL-CIO announced the contracts, Chavez ate grapes for the first time since he'd started the boycott five years earlier. "They were sweet grapes of justice," he said in his memoirs.

Workers joined UFWOC in waves, bringing the membership from a few thousand to at least 20,000 and by some estimates as many as 100,000. What's more, UFWOC worked out a deal with the Teamsters, who promised to stop recruiting farmworkers.

Nevertheless, the Teamsters refused to cancel the contracts that they had already signed with the lettuce growers. "This," Chavez told *Newsweek* magazine, "means all-out war." On August 24, he called on all California lettuce workers to go on strike. Within days, thousands of workers had walked out of the fields.

BEATINGS AND JAIL TIME

The day after Chavez called the strike, Jerry Cohen went with two aides and a journalist to speak with workers at the Hansen ranch, a Salinas-area farm. Cohen and his group found no one there but owner Al Hansen and at least six muscular thugs, one of whom was a 290-pound (130-kg) Teamster. When Hansen yelled, "Get 'em!", the men jumped the UFWOC group and beat them severely.

It was the first major attack in a strike that would be bloodier than anything UFWOC had ever encountered. Teamsters pummeled UFWOC picketers, threw rocks at them, whipped them with chains, drove cars into them, shot at them, broke their car windows with baseball bats, and threatened to blow up their homes. When one large grower, Inter Harvest, signed a contract with UFWOC, Teamster goons muscled into some of Inter Harvest's fields, blocked the workers from doing their jobs, and shut the fields down for days. Chavez's closest advisers told him to move with his family to a secret location so that the growers and Teamsters couldn't find and attack them. Chavez didn't like the idea but eventually went along with it.

On September 16, Salinas-area Superior Court Judge Anthony Brazil empowered the growers to ban picketing at their farms. At a press conference the next day, Chavez called off the picketing but called for a national boycott of non-UFWOC lettuce. "The boycott will be on until the last lettuce grower is signed up!"

To promote the boycott, Chavez went on tour. Soon, though, he wouldn't be free to travel at all, courtesy of lettuce grower Bud Antle.

Since 1961, the Teamsters had been Antle's union. When Chavez declared the lettuce boycott, Antle got a court order to block it. Chavez continued it anyway. On December 4, Salinas judge Gordon Campbell ordered Chavez jailed for contempt of court. As uniformed officers took Chavez to a cell, he shouted, "Boycott the hell out of them!"

By the time Campbell handed down his decision, thousands of Chavez's supporters had surrounded the courthouse. From then on, unionists and friends swarmed the courthouse to show their devotion to Chavez and his cause. Robert Kennedy's widow, Ethel, went to visit Chavez in prison, as did Martin Luther King, Jr.'s widow, Coretta. Both visits focused national attention on Chavez and strengthened the boycott.

To stop himself from brooding about being behind bars, Chavez decided to keep busy. He passed much of his time reading mail, which arrived in sacks.

Despite being jailed, Chavez remained defiant and encouraged people to continue the boycott.

The pressure to free Chavez apparently worked. On Christmas Eve, the authorities opened his cell and let him go. "My spirit was never in jail," Chavez told the throngs of supporters gathered outside. "They can jail us, but they can never jail the cause!"

The cause wasn't jailed, but it was moving—literally. While Chavez liked the Forty Acres, it was easy for people to reach, which meant there was an unending series of interruptions by people who wanted to see him. A sympathetic Hollywood producer helped the union acquire more than 200 acres (80 ha) in the pine-forested Tehachapi Mountains about 50 miles (80 km) southeast of Delano. By his forty-fourth birthday in March 1971, Chavez had moved the union's main offices into an old tuberculosis hospital on the premises. Helen Chavez had been a patient there as a child and didn't like moving the union headquarters there. Cesar, however, thought it was best for the organization.

Chavez named the place Nuestra Señora de la Paz (Our Lady of Peace), or La Paz for short. Some unionists felt that La Paz sheltered Chavez too much from his supporters, cutting him off from the outside world. The world got to him anyway.

In May of 1971, White House Counsel Charles Colson, President Nixon's chief lawyer, told the justice and labor departments to interfere in the Teamsters-UFWOC dispute "only if you can find some way to work against the Chavez union." In July, federal agents told Jerry Cohen that a group of growers had hired professional criminals to kill Chavez. The union hid Chavez again, to his annoyance. The criminals were later arrested.

In October, Larry Itliong resigned. As AWOC's former leader, UFWOC's vice president since 1966, and the man who had started the grape picker's strike, Itliong was UFWOC's second in command. He didn't feel like he was, though. He believed that Chavez and his closest allies had amassed too much power and were making decisions without consulting others. In particular, he felt that Chavez and company were more concerned with Mexican-American workers than with Filipinos like Itliong himself.

Chavez walks the grounds of La Paz, a place he hoped would be a peaceful headquarters for the union.

In March of 1972, the federal government's National Labor Relations Board (NLRB), which oversaw labor-management disputes, sued UFWOC to stop its secondary boycotts. Only after months of union protest demonstrations did the NLRB drop the suit.

BAD NEWS IN ARIZONA

The Grand Canyon State was tough on farmworkers. Arizona farmworkers averaged less than half the income of other Arizonans and were paid poorly even compared to other farmworkers. "The average hourly wage paid to Arizona farm workers was $1.70, as compared to $2.06 in the Pacific region and $1.84 nationally," wrote activist Joseph Mulligan in *America* magazine.

Working conditions were tough too. Arizona is one of the country's hottest and driest areas, and performing farmwork under its burning sun was not easy. Moreover, Arizona was a "right to work" state. In most states, an employee at a unionized workplace has to join the

From UFWOC to UFW

Amid all of UFWOC's troubles, many people didn't notice the quiet milestone that it reached in 1972. That year, UFWOC had more than 50,000 members, and by some estimates, more than 100,000. In February, the AFL-CIO decreed that the United Farm Workers Organizing Committee was more than just a group trying to organize a union. It was now a full-fledged union. Consequently, the union lopped off the last two words of its name and started calling itself the name it has had ever since: United Farm Workers, or UFW.

union. But in "right to work" states such as Arizona, workers don't have to join. This arrangement weakens the power of unions in negotiating with employers.

UFW had been trying to organize farmworkers in Arizona but hadn't made much progress. The state government favored the growers and feared that UFW could defeat them in Arizona as it had in California. The legislature wasn't about to let that happen. On May 12, 1972, it passed the Agricultural Employment Relations Act. The act took away almost all of UFW's strongest tools. It outlawed secondary boycotts and strikes at harvesttime (the most effective time to strike), restricted a union's right to picket employers, and forced workers who voted for a strike to keep working for sixty days before walking out. Any union that wanted to strike under these laws would find its strike too weak make the employer do anything.

Governor Jack Williams signed the act into law within an hour of its passage—an exceptionally quick move. Chavez was speaking at a rally against the act in Phoenix, the state capital. He tried to meet with Williams, but the governor refused to see him or other farmworker representatives. "As far as I'm concerned, these people do not exist," Williams said.

If Arizona could get away with antiunion laws, other states might pass similar laws and possibly weaken UFWOC to death. Chavez had to take a dramatic stand that would grab attention and sympathy. He declared a fast, which he called a "fast of love." What's more, he demanded a recall election to force Williams out of office. His supporters told him, *"No, se puede"*—"No, it can't be done." Chavez (or in one account, Dolores Huerta) answered *"Si, se puede!"*—"Yes, it can be done!" The three words became the union's new motto.

Chavez settled into bed in the Phoenix *barrio's* Santa Rita Community Center. A rise in his stomach acid level gave him stomach

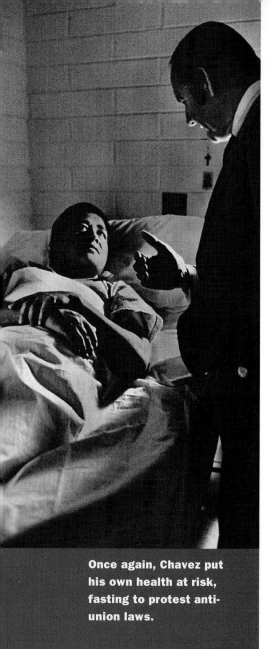

Once again, Chavez put his own health at risk, fasting to protest anti-union laws.

pain, but he kept starving himself. Even after his doctor hospitalized him near the end of May, he refused to eat. He kept participating in masses and other events, including meetings with Senator George McGovern, who soon became the Democratic candidate for president running against Richard Nixon.

By early June, Chavez's fast began to weaken his heart. Realizing that heart trouble could kill him, he called off the fast. On June 4, after spending more than three weeks without food, Chavez finally ate. He did it in front of thousands at a rally and mass, and he was so weak and nauseated that he stayed in bed until the moment he absolutely had to appear publicly. Immediately after he took his first bite of food, he went back to bed.

Chavez's pains didn't bring great results. Arizona didn't fire Jack Williams or repeal the farm law. Still, the recall drive did sign up plenty of new Latino voters who, in 1974, helped to elect Williams's successor, Raul Castro, the state's first Latino governor.

EIGHT

Decline and Revival

In some ways, Chavez and the UFW were riding high, especially in politics. At the Democratic National Convention in July 1972, Senator Edward Kennedy began his speech to the delegates by greeting them as "fellow lettuce boycotters," and the hall exploded with cheers. In California that same year, growers put an initiative on the ballot called Proposition 22, which was similar to Arizona's Agricultural Employment Relations Act. After a massive campaign by Chavez and his allies, voters rejected the proposition.

Chavez worked almost constantly, and his frequent travel to raise money or awareness for the union often kept him away from home. Still, he did try to keep close to his family. Helen and several of the children worked in the UFW's headquarters, walked picket lines, and otherwise supported Chavez's crusades. What's more, he tried to make time for family celebrations. In September of 1972, for instance, his first-born son Fernando got married. UFW supporter Anita Quintanilla attended the wedding and was surprised by the behavior of the world-famous union leader, hero to millions, and fighter against authority. "As I approached this family man for a dance," she reported years later, "the 'Chavez Mystique' vanished when I noticed how simple and down-to-earth he was. He shyly turned down my request."

After the wedding, it was back to work for Chavez. He and the UFW still had to fight the Teamsters, and the fight was getting tougher. The UFW

The Personal Side

Unlike the leaders of other unions, who earned more than $100,000 per year, Chavez took home about $5,000 in annual salary from the UFW. He led a humble life. He usually woke before dawn and did a series of yoga exercises. He wore the same type of same outfit every day: a simple work shirt, jeans, and white socks. He put in long hours, usually arriving at the UFW office well before any other worker, and often stayed late. He slept only three to five hours a night. To relax, he meditated or played with his dogs.

Though normally quiet and considerate, Chavez could burst into fits of temper, delivering harsh and angry scoldings at his subordinates. His fury, though, would subside quickly.

was hobbled. The court order banning boycotts that had gotten Chavez jailed was still in effect, preventing the union from enforcing the lettuce boycott by picketing stores that sold it. The court order stayed in effect until the California Supreme Court struck it down on December 29, 1972.

Meanwhile, the Teamsters were allying themselves with Chavez's opponents. Teamster president Frank Fitzsimmons was the only major union leader to support President Nixon for reelection in 1972. In December, Fitzsimmons became the first union boss to give a speech at the annual convention of the American Farm Bureau Federation, an anti-union growers' group. He offered to cooperate with the growers and take over the UFW's grape contracts.

Chavez couldn't believe it. "How can [the Teamsters] come in?" he asked a grower who told him about Fitzsimmons. "They don't represent the workers." By April 15, 1973, when the UFW's contracts with Coachella Valley grape growers expired, the Teamsters signed up more than 80 percent of the valley's fields, covering all but two growers—the liberal Lionel Steinberg and the like-minded K. K. Larson. The Teamster contracts eliminated UFW protection against pesticides, provided for a smaller raise in wages than the UFW wanted, and eliminated the union's hiring halls. (The growers hated the hiring halls, which often didn't deliver enough skilled workers.)

Chavez immediately called a strike. The next day, more than one thousand people were picketing Coachella Valley ranches.

The Teamsters brought in strikebreakers. They also brought in burly guards carrying baseball bats and other weapons, which they readily used on the picketers' cars and bodies. At least once a week, Teamsters bloodied UFW members.

Around the same time, local Superior Court Judge Fred Metheny issued an order against picketing. UFW supporters picketed anyway. Within a week, more than three hundred of them had been arrested.

Meanwhile, the Teamsters were moving into the San Joaquin Valley to take over the UFW's contracts when they expired in July. The first assault

The Teamsters' View

The Teamsters didn't care whether or not they had farmworkers' support, partly because they didn't respect the farmworkers. "It will be a couple of years before [workers] can start having membership meetings, before we can use the farmworkers' ideas in the union," Teamsters executive Einar Mohn told an interviewer in 1973. "I'm not sure how effective a union can be when it is composed of Mexican Americans and Mexican nationals with temporary visas."

came when the Teamsters signed up the immense E. & J. Gallo Winery, ending Gallo's six-year association with the UFW. Chavez immediately called a boycott and strike against Gallo and other anti-UFW growers. The AFL-CIO promised to give the UFW $1.6 million to help in the fight.

Nevertheless, the Teamsters marched on. By July 30, they had signed up nearly all of California's grape growers.

THE DEATH OF YOUNG AND OLD

Their victory didn't stop the attacks on picketers. Late at night on August 14, in one of the towns southeast of Delano, sheriff's deputy Gilbert Cooper clubbed twenty-four-year-old strike leader Nagi Daifullah with a heavy flashlight. The next night, Daifullah died. Two days after the assault, not many miles away, sixty-year-old UFW loyalist Juan de la Cruz was walking a vineyard picket line. Suddenly, five rifle

Members of the UFW protested the Teamsters' involvement in their dispute with Coachella Valley ranches.

shots burst from a pickup truck speeding past the picketers. One of the shots ripped through de la Cruz's chest and killed him.

A shocked and mournful Chavez instantly called off all picketing. Within a month, he cancelled the strike and redirected the union's efforts toward spreading across the United States and Canada to shore up the boycotts.

By late 1973, UFW membership had fallen to less than seven thousand. In 1973 and 1974, Chavez tried to negotiate peace with the Teamsters and get the California legislature to pass a farmworkers' rights law. Both efforts failed. He launched costly projects, such as lawsuits against the Teamsters and other opponents, that drained the union's treasury.

ON THE UPSWING

Outwardly, Chavez appeared confident. For many people, he was still a champion. When he visited Europe in September of 1974, even Pope

The protests turned deadly. The widow of Juan de la Cruz stands by her husband's coffin during his funeral. He was killed while walking on a picket line.

Paul VI wanted to meet him. During the meeting, which Chavez called one of the highlights of his life, the pope blessed Chavez's efforts and asked what *huelga* meant.

In late February of 1975, Chavez led a weeklong march from San Francisco to Gallo's headquarters in Modesto, more than 100 miles (160 km) away. More than fifteen thousand people eventually joined the march, and Governor Jerry Brown noticed.

California voters had elected Brown in November of 1974. He was Chavez's kind of politician, a liberal Democrat who had studied to become a Catholic priest. The two men had met in the late 1960s. After Brown had helped to fight Proposition 22 in 1972, Chavez had supported his run for the statehouse.

In the spring of 1975, Brown invited representatives of the UFW, Teamsters, AFL-CIO, and growers to his Sacramento apartment. Chavez sent lawyer Jerry Cohen to the meeting. On May 3, the group held what Chavez later called "the strangest meeting in the history of California

As a man with a Catholic upbringing, Chavez was delighted to meet the pope and receive his blessing.

Chavez would soon learn what could be accomplished with Governor Jerry Brown as a political ally.

agriculture." After two days and nights of negotiating, they emerged with a law, the Agricultural Labor Relations Act (ALRA).

Chavez liked the ALRA. It wasn't perfect; for one thing, it limited secondary boycotts. But it allowed unions to call strikes at harvesttime and established the Agricultural Labor Relations Board to hear disputes between employers and employees. Most importantly, it was the first law in U.S. history that empowered farmworkers to choose their own unions and kept growers from picking unions for them. It would go into effect on August 28.

Under the law, workers could sign petitions that would call for elections to choose which union to join. The Teamsters busily circulated petitions in fields where they expected to win the elections. To outdo them, Chavez set out on July 1 for his longest march ever: nearly 1,000 miles (1,600 km), starting at San Ysidro on the California side of the Mexican border.

With sixty other marchers, Chavez walked north to Sacramento, then south to La Paz. Virtually every night, the marchers held a rally to encourage workers to sign election petitions. The UFW estimated that during the march's fifty-nine days, Chavez spoke to more than eighty thousand workers.

The march seemed to revitalize him. Although Chavez was forty-eight years old, his back hurt, and the summer heat was sometimes brutal, he averaged more than 16 miles (25 km) a day—faster than his pace during the march to Sacramento, when he was nearly ten years younger.

Soon afterwards, another bit of good news came. The grape boycott was taking hold. In October of 1975, the Louis Harris polling organization found that 8 percent of U.S. adults were boycotting Gallo wines, 11 percent were boycotting lettuce, and 12 percent—17 million people—were boycotting grapes. It was a considerable show of Chavez's strength.

Would Chavez would be so strong in the fields? During 1976, more than forty thousand workers had held more than three hundred elections, but choosing an union wasn't an easy process. The underfunded Agricultural Labor Relations Board (ALRB), which was to certify the election results, ran out of money in early 1976 and closed its offices for months. Chavez fought for Proposition 14, a voter initiative that would have granted the ALRB more money, but in November 1976, the voters failed to accept it. Moreover, according to the UFW, Teamsters and growers interfered with voting and illegally blocked UFW organizers from talking to workers in the fields.

Nevertheless, Chavez's union won most of the elections. The Teamsters didn't take the results well. They said that the ALRB was biased toward the UFW. Governor Brown had appointed its board members, and most of them approved of Chavez and his union. Between the Teamsters and the UFW, "more than 80% of the elections were challenged," says *Cesar Chavez: A Triumph of Spirit*.

SAFE AT LAST?

Chavez had a scheme to resolve the disputes. For months, he and Jerry Cohen had been meeting secretly with Teamster leaders. On March 10, 1977, Chavez announced a peace treaty. "Both of us were fed up with fighting each other," Chavez explained.

The Teamsters agreed to stop signing up field-workers. They also agreed not to renew the contracts that they had already signed with growers. As he shook hands with his old enemy, Frank Fitzsimmons, Chavez smiled. "Now, the battle starts with the real opponents: the growers," he said.

Actually, though, the union cancelled some of its battles: the boycotts. Even though the Teamsters were pulling out of the fields and the UFW had more than fifty thousand members, public support for the boycotts was shriveling. On January 31, 1978, Chavez called the boycotts off. For the first time in nearly thirteen years, Chavez wasn't waging life-and-death fights with growers or Teamsters.

NINE

Losses

Chavez soldiered on. In June of 1978, he and Helen defied a court order against picketing an Arizona cantaloupe farm. He was arrested, convicted, and later released. In 1979, he helped Ohio's Farm Labor Organizing Committee wage a vegetable workers' strike and boycott against Campbell Soup Company. In the same year and into 1980, he joined California Assemblyman Howard Berman's campaign to become speaker of the Assembly (Berman lost). But his greatest effort of 1979 was the lettuce strike.

The lettuce growers' contracts with the UFW were due to expire, so Chavez was negotiating new ones. The growers wouldn't accept Chavez's demand that they raise wages by nearly 50 percent, from $3.70 to $5.25 an hour. On January 19, 1979, he declared a strike. It was the first strike that he had called just for wage increases, not for the right to negotiate.

Chavez had expected the strike to end quickly, without spreading far. He was wrong. The strike dragged on for months and eventually hit fields in the Imperial Valley, on both sides of the southern California–Arizona border. It even led to the death of striking worker Rufino Contreras, who, on February 10, was confronting some strikebreakers in a southern California lettuce field when ranch hands shot him in the chest.

Chavez didn't quit. Instead, he returned to using tactics that had worked before. In a press conference on April 26, he called on the people of the United States to boycott California lettuce.

Still, no growers met Chavez's demands until August 31, when Sun Harvest agreed to pay workers $5.00 an hour with automatic raises over the next two years, plus other benefits. After that, other growers slowly began to sign up with the UFW, but not all of them. Some of them held out and pushed the UFW away for years.

One holdout was Bruce Church, Inc., a grower of produce in Salinas, California, and southwestern Arizona. In July of 1983, Chavez launched a

Once again, Chavez had to battle the lettuce growers to improve the contracts for the farmworkers.

secondary boycott against one of the biggest buyers of Church's Red Coach brand of lettuce, the Lucky Stores supermarket chain.

This boycott was different from others that Chavez had run. It was a modern, high-tech advertising campaign. "We've got demographics and statistics people and professional direct-mail experts," he told United Press International reporter Timothy Elledge. The campaign's budget was $1 million, which came from donations and union dues.

SOUR TIMES

Though Chavez and the UFW looked strong, things were actually getting ugly within the union. In his memoirs, published in 1975, Chavez admitted, "The days when the union was *'una bella de guesto'*—just one happy bunch—are over."

Some union staff members fumed about specific incidents. Filipinos, for instance, were furious in July of 1977, when Chavez visited the Philippines and appeared pleased with Ferdinand Marcos, the islands' oppressive dictator. Other members resented the low wages that Chavez paid to union leaders.

Still other UFW officials disliked Chavez's use of The Game, which he introduced to the union around 1977. The Game was a form of psychotherapy that the antidrug organization Synanon used to make addicts see their problems clearly. In The Game, a circle of participants attacked each other's flaws with the most blunt and brutal words they could muster. Some UFW staff members found it painful to participate in The Game. Rather than slash into each other's weaknesses, they simply wanted to run the union's business.

The business needed running. A number of UFW members were upset that the union was inept at managing its medical insurance, credit union, and other benefit programs. The UFW was losing members, contracts with growers, and elections in the fields. It was losing money too. Even as it was reaching out to fewer and fewer workers, the UFW was giving more than $1 million to friendly politicians. In 1983, the California Fair Political Practices Commission fined the union $25,000 for giving these donations without reporting all of them to the state, as the laws required.

Meanwhile, the most radical of Chavez's Latino followers felt that he was too moderate. They denounced the United States as being ruled by white men who favored big business and were unhappy that Chavez rarely addressed the subject. What's more, they resented Chavez's reliance on white advisers, such as Jerry Cohen.

Even activists who were less radical wanted Chavez to keep *La Causa* going as a Latino political and social movement. That wasn't Chavez's plan. While he definitely wanted a better life for Latinos, he was

Chavez meets with workers during his visit to the Philippines, a trip that garnered a lot of criticism at home.

primarily a labor leader who called more often for fair wages and safe working conditions than for immigrants' rights or laws prohibiting discrimination.

The main complaint of most union officials, though, was that Chavez had become a tyrant. Other unions had local chapters that handled local workers. But that system, Chavez felt, didn't work for migrant workers, who never stayed in one place for long. Instead, Chavez controlled all the union's decisions himself. "If a car in Salinas needed a new tire, we had to check with Cesar," union staffer Aristeo Zambrano told writer Frank Bardacke of *The Nation* magazine.

For years, Chavez had been studying books about managing organizations, but he was not very skilled in managing people. Though he was often patient and kind, especially with young staffers, the years of attacks by Teamsters and growers had made him distrustful. He feared "malignant forces both in and out of the union who are jointly struggling to destroy our union," as he said at the UFW's September 1981 convention. In a 1977 issue of *The Nation*, former UFW staffer Michael Yates mentioned "Chavez's need to have absolute control over the union and the unquestioning loyalty of its members," and added, "Those who criticize him are perceived as threats to himself and to the union." Chavez seemed to have shifted from disagreeing with more radical unionists to actively rejecting them. When Zambrano and eight other worker representatives opposed Chavez's choices for the UFW executive board in September of 1981, Chavez fired them.

They weren't the only ones. "Some of us former staff members joke that Chavez should be listed in the *Guinness Book of World Records* under 'Most Firings,'" UFW employee Susan Drake wrote in an article for *The*

Progressive magazine. As early as April of 1976, said Michael Yates, "virtually all of my friends [at the union] had been fired or had quit; the union's central staff had been reduced by more than a third." By 1981, even such stalwarts, or strong supporters, as Jerry Cohen had left.

Chavez lost his most powerful political ally as well. In November 1982, California voters replaced Jerry Brown with the conservative George Deukmejian. Cornell University professor of farm labor Clete

On the Radio

Not everything went wrong for Chavez and the UFW. In 1983, Chavez founded Radio Campesina, a radio station for farmworkers. The station started out in Visalia, about 37 miles (60 km) north of Delano, nearly the center of California. At first, it broadcast "all talk, the delivery dry and earnest," wrote journalist Ingrid Lobet in 2000. Even when it played music, the songs were "South American protest music for older Chicanos rather than music for immigrants," according to Chavez's son Paul, who with his brother Anthony took over the station in the late 1980s.

After they took it over, the brothers revitalized the station. They played music that appealed to young workers, with lively announcers and a memorable slogan: *"Buenos tardes! Es Campesina, y no maaasssss!"* ("Good afternoon! It's Campesina, and nothing ellllsssse!").

The new format worked. Campesina expanded into a network of several small stations. Still, the network never forgot its roots. Campesina began every broadcast day with a prayer: "Lord, give me honesty and patience . . . so that we will never tire of the struggle." The author of the prayer was Cesar Chavez.

Daniel called Deukmejian "unarguably the opponent of farmworker organizing and a reliable friend of the growers."

STIRLING SHIFTS DIRECTION

Shortly after taking office in January 1983, Deukmejian appointed former assemblyman M. David Stirling as the ALRB's general counsel. Stirling's job was to choose which worker complaints against growers to submit to the board for action.

"When I got here, the place reeked of a bias toward one union, that being the United Farm Workers," Stirling told *New York Times* reporter Katherine Bishop. Whether or not that was true, Stirling changed things. Before 1983, General Counsels Harry Delizonna and Walter Kintz submitted about 35 percent of all worker complaints to the board; by August 1985, Stirling was submitting only about 10 percent. In 1982, about four hundred complaints from farmworkers were backlogged, waiting for General Counsel Delizonna to investigate them. In 1984, under Stirling, the number rose above one thousand.

In June 1984, when Deukmejian cut the ALRB's budget and weakened the board even further, Chavez was furious. Within weeks, he announced a new boycott of California-grown grapes. "We take this action because under Deukmejian, the law that guarantees our right to organize has been shut down."

The boycott didn't take hold. Bruce Obbink, president of a growers' group called the California Table Grape Commission, told *USA Today*'s Barbara Reynolds, "In 1985, we shipped 59.6 million boxes of table grapes, which was the largest table-grape crop in the history of the grape business."

Chavez gives a press conference, alerting the media and the general public about the health hazards associated with pesticides.

FROM BOYCOTT TO PESTICIDES

In the summer of 1985, Chavez switched strategies. Since the 1960s, he had attacked grape growers for making workers spray harmful pesticides on crops. He now emphasized that problem, making the boycott about life and death instead of wages. He had good reason. In 1984, the small grape-growing town of McFarland faced a mystery. Located about 10 miles (16 km) south of Delano, with a population of less than seven thousand, McFarland suffered an abnormally high cancer rate, especially among children. "From 1975 through 1984, thirteen children were diagnosed with cancer and six died," said a Stanford University report. "This incidence of cancer was eight times the national average." Growers near McFarland had been spraying their crops with the pesticide methyl bromide, among other things.

The news of the McFarland cancer cluster, as well as similar clusters in other San Joaquin Valley farm towns, brought an enormous amount of attention to the pesticide problem. Chavez and the UFW sent millions of letters to possible supporters, asking for help. One letter, signed by farmworker Manuel Amaya, said, "My oldest son writes this letter to you because I cannot. My right hand was lost to infection from the poisons in the fields."

In addition, the union produced a short film, *The Wrath of Grapes*, that showed the effects of pesticides. It included shots of deformed children and desperately ill farmworkers. Chavez traveled the country, showing the film and giving speeches to help uphold the boycott. Along the way, he pointed out that the pesticides could remain on fruits and vegetables, and sicken people who ate them.

Chavez's new direction earned him and the boycott a lot of publicity. Newspapers and national magazines reported his charges, and some politicians tried to outlaw the most dangerous pesticides. For the most part, though, growers continued spraying the chemicals on their plants.

IRCA AND YUMA

Chavez got some additional bad news on November 6, 1986, when Congress passed the Immigration Reform and Control Act (IRCA). Like the *bracero* program, IRCA let growers bring in low-wage, nonunion workers from out of the country. Chavez protested the law, but it didn't change.

Possibly the worst blow to the UFW was delivered on April 6, 1988, when a Superior Court judge in Yuma ordered the UFW to pay $5.4 million to Bruce Church, Inc. The case stemmed from Chavez's 1983 boycott of Lucky Stores that were carrying Church's lettuce.

Church said that the Lucky boycott violated Arizona's 1972 Agricultural Employment Relations Act, which outlawed secondary boycotts.

Chavez couldn't believe the ruling. "How can a rural Arizona court award damages for a boycott which occurred in California?" he asked. The judgment hurt the UFW badly. The union no longer had much money. The number of dues-paying members had dropped by two-thirds since the early 1980s. Even worse, the grape boycott was no longer working. Most people in the United States had stopped caring about it. Chavez needed to make them care again.

THE LAST FAST

On July 16, 1988, Chavez stopped eating. He explained that he was fasting to protest "the terrible suffering of farm workers and their children, the crushing of farm-worker rights, the denial of fair and free [union] elections, and the death of good-faith collective bargaining [between growers and workers] in California agriculture."

The fast was also a way to punish himself and others for not doing more to help farmworkers and their families who were suffering with cancer. "Do we feel their pain deeply enough?" he asked in a statement he issued on July 26. "I know I don't, and I'm ashamed." In another statement, he added that he was fasting to atone "for those in positions of moral authority and for all men and women activists who know what is right and just, who know that they could or should do more."

At the end of his last major fast, his doctors warned that another bout of starvation could kill him. That was in 1972, when he was forty-four years old. Now, Chavez was sixty-one, and the fast hit him hard. In the first eight days, he lost about 15 pounds (7 kg). By the eighteenth day, he was verging on severe kidney damage. "It took a toll on us, that fast," Chavez's daughter Linda said in *The Fight in the Fields*. "It was scary. [Chavez's] grandkids were very upset." Even worse, the fast wasn't achieving much. Chavez wasn't talking to reporters, so the fast didn't get much media attention.

Things changed a bit in early August, when three of Robert Kennedy's adult children came to Delano. Wherever Kennedys went, the press followed. On August 4, they joined Chavez at an evening mass attended by hundreds of people.

The Kennedy publicity helped the boycott. A few days later, seven labor unions in Florida promised to boycott grapes. Soon, other unions joined in.

Still, Chavez didn't quit. By August 6, he was dehydrated and malnourished, and often dizzy or nauseous. His blood pressure was rising, a sign that heart damage was probably beginning. By August 11, he had lost about 30 pounds (14 kg), suffered from stomach cramps, and could barely stand. His doctors predicted that he couldn't fast much longer without dying. Yet he still refused to eat.

Reverend Jesse Jackson, a presidential candidate and an ally of Chavez's, came to Delano on August 14 to talk him out of fasting. Jackson offered to keep Chavez's fast going by taking it up himself and then handing it off to others.

Chavez agreed but didn't stop fasting right away. He grew weaker and sicker. If he was trying to get pesticides off fruit, his efforts were failing. Some people picketed markets that sold grapes, but consumers didn't boycott in numbers large enough to make the growers stop spraying.

At last, on August 21, more than six thousand farmworkers came to the Forty Acres. So did Jackson and the trio of young Kennedys and their mother, Ethel. Chavez's sons Paul and Anthony helped their fragile father to a chair on a platform. On either side sat Ethel Kennedy and Cesar's ninety-six-year-old mother, Juana. Ethel Kennedy shared a Catholic communion with Chavez by handing him a small piece of bread. Chavez's last major campaign was over.

Chavez's last fast took an enormous toll on his health. Reverend Jesse Jackson met with Chavez, hoping to convince him to end the fast.

Death and Rebirth

Recovering from the 1988 fast took Chavez weeks. Eventually, though, he returned to his usual schedule of endless work. He traveled all over California to picket supermarkets, raise funds for the UFW, and give speeches. By the middle of 1989, he was traveling the East Coast to form alliances with various unions and enlist their support for the boycott. Possibly because of the other unions' help, sales of grapes fell in several major cities during 1990.

Chavez made progress on other fronts as well. In April of 1990, he went to Mexico and signed an agreement with President Carlos Salinas de Gortari to provide medical benefits to Mexicans working in the United States. It was a considerable achievement, as most of the workers weren't getting health insurance from U.S. companies or the U.S. government. Seven months later, President Salinas de Gortari awarded

Chavez the Order of the Aztec Eagle, Mexico's highest honor, for "efforts in defense of the human rights of Mexican nationals in the United States."

Yet in some ways, Chavez's fame was shrinking. When he appeared with supporters and allies such as Reverend Jesse Jackson or the popular Latino band Los Lobos, the crowds and the press gave them more attention than they gave to Chavez and his causes.

TWO DEATHS

On December 14, 1991, Chavez's mother died of kidney failure. He held in his emotions at the funeral but made no public appearances until February of 1992, when the UFW held a convention. Even then, he didn't put in as much time as he had at previous meetings. He surfaced in April with Jesse Jackson at a rally for jobs in Los Angeles. In June, he returned to the Coachella Valley to speak at a union rally. The next month, he led more than ten thousand workers through the Salinas area in a march demanding higher wages and better treatment.

Just as he was ramping up to full activity, another tragedy hit. On September 27, Fred Ross died of cancer. The two men had been friends for forty years. In the eulogy he gave at Ross's funeral, Chavez said, "The thing I liked most about Fred was there were … no pretensions, no ego gimmicks. Just plain, hard work—at times, grinding work. I shall miss him very much."

Ross's death didn't pull Chavez away from work as his mother's death had. In November and December, for instance, he visited New York City and San Francisco to gather support for his grape boycott. In

April of 1993, he went to Yuma, Arizona, to testify in a retrial of the Bruce Church lawsuit.

ONE MORE LOSS

During the trip, Chavez stayed at the home of a friend and retired farmworker in San Luis, a small town about 20 miles (32 km) south of Yuma and 25 miles (40 km) southwest of the farm where Chavez had spent his boyhood. On April 22, 1993, after he had finished the day's testimony, he was in good spirits. He ate his usual vegetarian dinner, exercised, and lay down to read about Native American art.

The next morning, when Chavez hadn't come to breakfast, David Martinez went to get him. Martinez, a UFW activist traveling with Chavez, found him on his bed, fully clothed, his reading material close at hand. He was dead.

The exact cause of Chavez's death was never publicly revealed, but "we didn't see any signs that he had been through any pain," Martinez told the *Los Angeles Times*'s Patrick McDonnell. Some people who knew Chavez suspected that his fasts may have shortened his life.

Martinez started calling Chavez's family and friends. "We're in a state of shock," Dolores Huerta confessed to *Los Angeles Times* writer George Ramos. "His mother was 99 when she died. His father was 101. All of his family has longevity. So no one ever anticipated Cesar having an early death."

"I'm very sad. He was one of the most important labor leaders since World War II," said Jerry Brown. "He stood apart from the rest. He stressed the need for cooperation. . . . He wanted to give power to the powerless."

Even the California Table Grape Commission's Bruce Obbink was polite. "He committed himself wholeheartedly to a cause he believed to be worthy and just, and he pursued his quest tirelessly. We regret the loss to his family and friends."

Government offices in Los Angeles and Sacramento lowered their flags to half-mast. In Oxnard's La Colonia *barrio*, hundreds of mourners gathered near Chavez's boyhood home and marched through town to honor his memory. The governments of Denver, Boston, Illinois, Ohio,

Presidential Proclamation

On the day of Chavez's funeral, President Bill Clinton issued a proclamation to celebrate Chavez's life. Part of it read:

Cesar Chavez came from the humble yet proud beginnings of a migrant worker to lead those same workers in a movement that irreversibly shaped our Nation. . . . Inspired by the teachings of a Catholic priest and by the writings of Gandhi and other great civil leaders, Cesar rose to become one of the great labor leaders of our time. . . .

Cesar's innate understanding of the problems facing migrant workers allowed him to organize thousands of farmworkers across the Nation. With natural leadership and unflagging determination, he achieved real progress where others had failed.

His insistence on nonviolent tactics stood in stark contrast to the bitterness and brutality that were used [by others]. The strength of his vision and the power of his leadership enabled him to take his struggle directly to the American people. He focused our Nation's attention on the economic and social plight of migrant farmworkers and, in the process, taught us how injustice anywhere affects us everywhere.

Minnesota, and Colorado issued resolutions recognizing his accomplishments.

On April 29, more than thirty thousand people—mostly farmworkers and their families—marched in Chavez's funeral procession from downtown Delano to the Forty Acres. Some of them carried the plain pine coffin that Chavez had asked his brother Richard to build.

By the end of 1995, more than twenty schools had been named after him. A dozen cities named streets for him. Eleven organizations created scholarships in his name. The states of California and New Mexico, and nearly a dozen cities and counties—seven in California alone—declared his birthday a holiday.

Still, hard feelings lived on. When the city of Fresno named a street after Chavez, some people objected so strongly that the city changed the street's name. In Delano, which proudly displays a number of historical markers, only one place—a quiet park—is named after the town's most famous citizen.

RODRIGUEZ'S REVIVAL

As for the UFW, Chavez had made a prediction. "If the union falls apart when I am gone, I will have been a miserable failure."

He wasn't. His son-in-law Arturo Rodriguez, a longtime UFW official, succeeded him as the union's president. Rodriguez refocused the UFW's efforts toward organizing workers, winning field elections, and negotiating with growers. "The Texas-born son of a sheet-metal worker has transformed the stagnant UFW into the fastest-growing union in the country," *Time* magazine's Margot Hornblower wrote in November

1996. By the end of 1997, the union's membership had grown from the 20,000 that it had at Chavez's death to more than 25,000—an increase of more than 20 percent.

The union even reached a truce with Bruce Church, Inc. In early 1996, an Arizona court reviewing the Church–UFW lawsuit declared that the union didn't have to pay the $5.4 million judgment. In the spring, Bruce Church, Inc. signed a contract for the UFW to represent its workers.

THE LIVING LEGACY

No matter how much the UFW accomplished after Chavez's death, no one can forget the achievements of his life. As he said in a 1984 speech to San Francisco's prestigious Commonwealth Club, "All my life, I have been driven by one dream, one goal, one vision: To overthrow a farm labor system in this nation which treats farm workers as if they were not important human beings."

Before the UFW, no union had ever won the right to represent farmworkers on a large scale and for a long time period. He secured rights for farmworkers that even some workers themselves thought were unattainable. He obtained rest periods for workers during the workday and clean drinking water and toilet facilities in the fields. He got bans on the uses of certain pesticides. His union's health-insurance and credit-union benefits gave farmworkers security and protection from crises, and allowed them to dream of an old age filled with peace rather than sickness and death caused by overwork.

More important, though, was Chavez's role as a leader. Millions of Latinos, farmworkers, and others endured endless poverty and vicious discrimination. The world treated them as if they were worthless. Then along came a man who lived like them, worked like them, and suffered like them. He told them that they weren't worthless and that they deserved fair treatment. He ordered the world to give them respect and a decent way of life, and eventually the world listened. He was a hero.

In 2002, on the seventy-fifth anniversary of Chavez's birth, newspapers reported honors for Chavez ranging from government tributes to a new rose. The Cesar Chavez rose was being developed by management and UFW-represented workers at Bear Creek Farms in Wasco, California. The farms were not far from the fields that Cesar's National Farm Workers Association had picketed in their first strike thirty-seven years earlier.

Cesar Chavez's dream can be summed up by his statement, "From the depth of need and despair, people can work together, can organize themselves to solve their own problems, and fill their own needs with dignity and strength."

The UFW continues Chavez's work today. UFW president Arturo Rodriguez, actor Martin Sheen, and Chavez's daughter, Sylvia Chavez Delagando, participate in a march to celebrate the UFW's fortieth anniversary.

Timeline

1927 Cesario Estrada Chavez, better known as Cesar Chavez, is born on March 31.

1929 Worldwide economic depression begins.

1937 To collect on debts that his father Librado Chavez owes, the government takes over the Chavez family farm on August 29.

1938 The Chavez family leaves the farm and joins Librado in the southern California farm town of Oxnard during the late summer.

1939 World War II begins.

1939–1944 The Chavezes travel California as migrant farmworkers.

1941 The United States enters World War II.

1943 Early in the year, Chavez meets Helen Fabela at La Baratita, a malt shop in Delano, California.

1944 Chavez joins the U.S. Navy.

1945 World War II ends.

1946 The navy discharges Chavez, who returns to farmwork.

1948 Chavez marries Helen Fabela on October 22.

1952 Chavez begins to help activist Fred Ross run a voter-registration drive and organize new Community Service Organization (CSO) chapters.

1962 Chavez quits the CSO in March. From April to September, he lays the groundwork for the National Farm Workers Association (NFWA). The first NFWA convention takes place on September 30.

1965 Grape pickers of the Agricultural Workers Organizing Committee (AWOC) in Delano go on strike to demand higher wages on September 8. NFWA votes to help AWOC in its strike on September 16. Cesar launches a boycott against Schenley Industries, a major San Joaquin Valley winemaker, in mid-December.

1966 To publicize the Schenley boycott, Chavez and others start a march from Delano to California's capital, Sacramento, on March 17. During the summer, NFWA and AWOC merge into United Farm Workers Organizing Committee (UFWOC).

1967 UFWOC calls a strike and boycott at Giumarra Vineyards.

1968 UFWOC calls for a boycott of all California table grapes in January. Chavez begins a fast to unite his union in nonviolent protest on February 14. Before thousands of witnesses, Chavez breaks his fast on March 10.

Civil rights leader Martin Luther King Jr. is assassinated on April 4. Robert F. Kennedy is assassinated on June 4.

1969 Chavez kicks off a secondary boycott of grapes with a 100-mile (160-km) march from Indio to Calexico in southern California from May 10 to May 18.

1970 Growers start signing contracts with UFWOC in the spring and summer. In the summer, UFWOC works to organize farmworkers in California's lettuce-growing Salinas and Santa Maria areas, and runs into opposition from the Teamsters union. Chavez calls a lettuce strike on August 24.

1971 In July, federal agents tell UFWOC lawyer Jerry Cohen that a group of growers has hired criminals to kill Chavez.

1972 UFWOC changes its name to United Farm Workers (UFW) in February. Chavez begins a fast on May 13. Chavez breaks his fast in front of thousands of supporters on June 4.

Arizona passes the Agricultural Employment Relations Act, which outlaws secondary boycotts and harvesttime strikes, on May 12.

1973 UFW contracts with Coachella Valley grape growers expire on April 15. The Teamsters sign up more than 80 percent of the valley's fields. Chavez immediately calls a strike and eventually a boycott.

1974 Chavez tries to negotiate peace with the Teamsters and get the California legislature to pass a farmworkers' rights law. Both efforts fail.

Impeachment hearings against President Richard Nixon begin in May. He resigns on August 9.

1975 In May, representatives of the UFW, Teamsters, and growers meet with Governor Jerry Brown to negotiate the Agricultural Labor Relations Act. The law grants unprecedented rights to farmworkers and creates the Agricultural Labor Relations Board (ALRB) to enforce their rights.

1977 Chavez announces a peace treaty with the Teamsters on March 10.

1979 Chavez declares a strike against lettuce growers to try and attain higher wages on January 19. To jump-start the sagging strike, Chavez calls on the people of the United States on April 26 to boycott California lettuce.

1982 California voters elect the conservative, anti-UFW George Deukmejian governor in November.

1983 Chavez launches a secondary boycott against lettuce grower Bruce Church, Inc. and Lucky Stores in July.

1984 On July 11, Chavez announces a new boycott of California-grown grapes to protest Deukmejian's gutting of the ALRB.

1985 In the summer, Chavez uses the grape boycott to emphasize the dangers of pesticides.

1988 On April 6, a Superior Court judge in Yuma, Arizona, orders the UFW to pay $5.4 million to Bruce Church, Inc. for violating the Agricultural Employment Relations Act. To strengthen the grape boycott, Chavez launches a fast on July 16. Chavez breaks the fast before more than six thousand people on August 21.

1992 In the Salinas area during July, Chavez leads more than ten thousand people in a march to demand higher wages and better treatment for farmworkers.

1993 On April 23, while in Arizona on a visit to testify in a retrial of the Bruce Church, Inc. lawsuit, Chavez dies.

To Find Out More

BOOKS

Drake, Susan Samuels. *Fields of Courage: Remembering Cesar Chavez & the People Whose Labor Feeds Us.* Santa Cruz, California: Many Names Press, 1999.

Ferriss, Susan, and Ricardo Sandoval. *The Fight in the Fields: Cesar Chavez and the Farmworkers Movement.* New York: Harcourt, 1997.

Griswold del Castillo, Richard, and Richard A. Garcia. *Cesar Chavez: A Triumph of Spirit.* Norman, Oklahoma: University of Oklahoma Press, 1995.

Mooney, Patrick H., and Theo J. Majka. *Farmers' and Farm Workers' Movements: Social Protest in American Agriculture.* New York: Twayne Publishers, 1995.

ORGANIZATIONS AND ONLINE SITES

Cesar E. Chavez Foundation
500 North Brand Boulevard, Suite 1650
Glendale, CA 91203
http://www.cesarechavezfoundation.org

The foundation's mission is to improve communities by preserving, promoting, and applying the legacy and values of Cesar Chavez.

Cesar E. Chavez Institute
San Francisco State University
3004 16th Street #301
San Francisco, CA 94103
http://www.sfsu.edu/~cecipp/cesar_chavez/chavezhome.htm

The institute is dedicated to studying and documenting the impact of social oppression on the health, education, and well-being of ethnic minority communities in the United States.

Si Se Puede! Cesar E. Chavez and His Legacy
http://clnet.ucr.edu/research/chavez/ or
latino.sscnet.ucla.edu/research/chavez/

This site offers an online exhibit that commemorates and documents Cesar Chavez's contribution to the California labor movement and his dedication to the use of nonviolence in fighting for social justice.

United Farm Workers
PO Box 62
Keene, CA 93531
http://www.ufw.org

This is the Web site of the union that Chavez founded, which is still in operation and dedicated to helping farmworkers.

A Note on Sources

One challenge in writing a book on Cesar Chavez is the immense stacks of magazine stories, newspaper articles, books, Web sites, and other items that report on his life. The years of his greatest fame were also years of great journalism, and a lot of it centered on Chavez.

The best book about Chavez is *Cesar Chavez: Autobiography of La Causa* by Jacques Levy. It includes extensive first-person accounts by Chavez, Dolores Huerta, Fred Ross, and several of Chavez's relatives, and contains information that's available nowhere else. Two books written by journalists who accompanied Chavez during the most eventful times of his life, *Delano* by John Gregory Dunne and *Sal Si Puedes: Cesar Chavez and the New American Revolution* by Peter Matthiessen, deliver eyewitness tales of Chavez's activities and insights on the world around him. Of the writers who looked at Chavez in historical perspective, the best include Susan Ferriss and Ricardo Sandoval, authors of *The Fight in the Fields: Cesar Chavez and the Farmworkers Movement*.

It's a shame that Harry Bernstein never wrote a book about Chavez. As the *Los Angeles Times*'s top labor reporter, he covered Chavez's adventures and provided a deep understanding of the issues that Chavez tackled. The *San Francisco Chronicle*'s Dick Meister and *The Nation*'s Ronald B. Taylor also wrote great stories that threw light on Chavez and his crusades. To find other newspaper and magazine articles, I consulted the databases LexisNexis, Infotrac, and ProQuest, and multivolume books such as *The Reader's Guide to Periodical Literature*.

The life of a man who traveled as often as Chavez did meant consulting plenty of maps. The best for my purposes was Thomas Brothers' *California Road Atlas & Driver's Guide*. For facts of all kinds, I turned to my encyclopedias: *Collier's Encyclopedia* and the Grolier *Encyclopedia of Knowledge*.

The Internet was a plentiful source of information. For information about Chavez and his union, the United Farm Workers' site was helpful. The search engines Google and AlltheWeb helped me dig up facts about everything else.

Finally, I am fortunate to have lived in California all my life, so I had a running start in understanding Chavez's world. In addition, I visited the San Joaquin Valley, including Delano, the Forty Acres, and other places where Chavez lived and worked. There's nothing like walking in a man's footsteps to help you understand his life.

—*David Seidman*

Index

About the Author

David Seidman is the author of more than twenty books, including *Secret Service Agents*, *Civil Rights*, *The Young Zillionaire's Guide to Supply and Demand*, *Secret Agent!*, *Exploring Careers in Journalism*, *All Gone: Things That Aren't There Anymore*, *U.S. Warplanes: F/A-18C Hornet*, and *Wonders of the World*. He is nowhere near as scholarly as you might expect from that list of books.